Sound in the Gospel: for the knucklehead tech in all of us

by David Lee Wright
Edited & Formatted by Beatriz G. Wright

Published by NEBTHOS
www.nebthos.com

Author Photo: Katherine J Photography

For permissions contact:
book@soundinthegospel.com

Published September 19th, 2016

ISBN: 978-0-692-77279-9

Printed in the United States of America

This book is dedicated to the memory of Paul Rice,
who told me a long time ago...

That it really IS all about GAIN.

Table of Contents

Acknowledgements

Thanks to my wonderful wife Bea, without whom this book would not be possible. Thank you for the endless hours of editing and listening to me as I tried to process this thing.

I couldn't have done it without you.

I truly love you to the moon and back!

Matt, Tyler, Zach, and Jon. Thanks for all the van conversations and late night Waffle House trips, for all the scattered beams, and the "Mers" in between.

I've been blessed with incredible mentors and friends who have helped me to grow as a sound tech over the years. Andy Sykora, Bill Park, Todd Saverence, Lin Clegg, Jon Lee, Shane Allison, Trey Maxwell, Kevin Jolly, Jay Leary, Ben Clark, Doug Martleon, David Bailey, and so many countless others.

Much appreciation to Cornerstone Church, The Summit Church, Grace Community Church, Bridge Community Church, Triangle Community Church, and the many venues that have ever hosted us.

To everyone who helped us proof the book: you have no idea how much it helped. We are forever grateful.

Special Thanks: Tim Keeler, Brandon Dean, David Harrell, Matt Moore, Brian Self, Daniel Lowe, Daniel Sigmon, and Matt Carter.

Shout out to David and Nick. "The Endless River" has been the go-to soundtrack while writing this book.

Thanks to Tom and Bea Eisenhour (and clan) for embracing me as family and encouraging us through this process and our marriage.

And finally, thanks to my parents, Dean and Phyllis Wright, for their love and support throughout my life.

Foreword

The truth is that in churches and conferences across America today, <u>worship has become more about a product we produce than a God who consumes us.</u> Our technical mastery at 'pulling-off' the experience on a professional level is not something that should be categorically condemned, but the cog-in-a-wheel pragmatics of it all….the monotony of 'doing' church at such an exhausted pace…. this needs to be shaken. Which is why I am so glad Dave has written what he has. "If you want to build a ship," says French writer and poet Antoine Marie de Saint-Exupéry….

> don't drum up people to collect wood and don't assign them tasks and work…but rather teach them to long for the endless immensity of the sea.
> —*The Endless Immensity*

This is why we do ministry…this is why we turn knobs on a sound board on Sundays. God is good, God is true, and God is beautiful. And eternity hangs in the balance. Much can be and should be said about being more efficient and effective in the practical arenas we serve in. And Dave does some of that here.

But exhaustion and disillusionment are inevitable unless we find ourselves again and again at a well. At a vision. So I am delighted that there is a relentlessness in these pages about bringing us back to the 'why's' of worship. And that 'why' is the gospel. The gospel, Dave reminds us, is what shapes our worship both on a corporate level and on a personal level.

On a corporate level…..music, sound, all these things are supposed to serve the purpose of adorning something…someone…. they are not the central thing. And that someone is not anyone on a stage or behind a board. That someone is Jesus Christ and that something is the gospel.

To be a minister of worship is to be a John the Baptist who, when he received the attention, immediately aimed it away from himself, saying, "Behold, the Lamb of God." We worship a God who is simultaneously beyond us and with us. Songs are great, but they are not enough. Sound is great, but it is not enough.

We were made for God. But this is true also on a personal level, which is another reason I am so thankful for this book. Dave presents a delightful mixture of theological and pastoral truth in these pages. He reminds us that where we find our identity, personally, is what we are truly worshiping. Many of us, myself especially, tend to believe "we are what we do" or "we are how we perform."

This leads to defensiveness when we think people are questioning us. It leads to anxiety, resentment, and eventually despair because we aren't perfect! But the gospel tells us we are loved and accepted before we do anything, and this truth changes everything. The gospel says we are already approved, already rich in Christ, already secure…and so there is no longer anything to prove.

We don't need praise. We don't need everyone to thank us anymore. This, needless to say, changes everything about the spirit and posture in which we serve. If ministry is my identity, criticism will shake me, and praise will make me. If God is my identity, I'll be able to take criticism, receive what's true about it, and move forward. If God is my identity, I'll be able to hear praise, humbly say 'thank you', and thank the God who gives every good gift. Dave uses scripture and stories to beautifully weave together this one of a kind book that I'm certain will be helpful to many, many churches and ministries.

I couldn't recommend this book highly enough. If your ministry is in the rut of monotony, or if it is in stuck in paralyzing idealism, Dave is a voice of reason, encouragement, and most of all, a voice of vision…relentlessly calling us to zoom out, take a deep breath, and remember Who worship is really all about.

Matt Papa
Recording Artist, Songwriter, Author of *Look & Live*

Introduction

I don't know how this book found its way into your hands. Maybe someone let you borrow it, maybe your worship leader emphatically begged you to read it, maybe you found it covered in dust, hidden under the sound board. Maybe you found it in a bin labeled "Things to Recycle" or just "BURN." Or maybe you actually bought this book. Then, HOORAY! I actually sold a book! And you can give me an invisible high five through time and space! YES! Well, I'm pleased to meet you, whoever you are. My name is Dave. My friends call me Magic Dave. And to answer your first question, "No."

The nickname came from my ability to twist knobs and reconnect cables until things worked. Nine times out of ten, I really didn't even do anything to fix it in the first place (which strangely happens more often than you'd think). But the name stuck. I hope you won't tell anyone my secret.

I got my start in sound production over 10 years ago. I was attending Kentucky Christian College, as it was known then. I was in a band and I wanted to record said band which, thankfully, was not recorded. I was introduced to a man by the name of Paul Rice who encouraged me to "get my live sound legs before I jumped into studio sound." Paul was the seasoned sound engineer at KCC and was not only a beast of a bass player and accomplished musician all around, but a GEEK of a man. He loved everything from Monty Python to SpongeBob SquarePants.

He was a counselor to wayward freshman, a relationship guru, maker of men, and friend to all concerned. Paul just loved people. And to one particular senior with four months to graduate, God would use this man to 180 my life. I was going to be a history teacher, but Paul made me want to be a sound engineer. I would stick around KCC for the following eight months running sound with Paul, learning everything I could. After graduation, I started a journal to use like a scrapbook for all the sound productions I would be a part of in the future. Paul wrote me a message on the first page and I would like to share it with you (see opposite page).

Words to live by indeed. The bit about bacon has proven itself painfully true.

I've been running sound for different churches, production companies, and touring bands for over 14 years now. I've learned a lot, thanks to the foundation Paul laid for me, but I've also made A LOT of mistakes. I've blown up my fair share of amps, speakers, monitors, tweeters, sound boards, and worship leaders.

I would like to address upfront that I really don't know everything there is to running sound, and I'm not sure anyone can say they know everything…except for a few chosen gurus that come down from on high, twist one knob and fix everything.

That being said, this book is not an exhaustive technical manual of how to run sound. The toolbox section in the latter half of this book is there to get you and your sound system in the ballpark (which I hope you will come to see as a good thing sometimes) and to help those who have basic questions, fears, and doubts. I realize that production talk can sound like Klingon to some, so I have included a glossary as well, which is roughly arranged alphabetically by topic.

As a side note, I completely understand that sound engineers, musicians, etc can be men or women, but to make life easier, most

Dave,

Run! Save Yourself while you still have time! Run away — run away!

So, you decided to stay Oh, Well!

Three things to remember,
Crap going in is only louder crap,
It's all about GAIN,
Never fry bacon in the nude.

It has been a singular pleasure, pure and simple, to be your acquaintance.
Yo — your friend
God bless your ears

Paul Rico

of the referential pronouns are written in the general "he" format. This in no way means that I do not approve of or value women in these positions. Please don't send me angry letters. (It was actually my wife's idea.)

For the first half of this book, we are going to address the heart of the sound engineer. And that doesn't just mean "have a good attitude and smile." We're going to look at what it's like to walk out the gospel in what is likely one of the most stressful positions in the church body today.

So, let's zoom out for a moment and think about what it is that we actually do as a sound person on Sunday. Sure, we come in, set things up, turn on the board, twist some knobs and push the faders, and mix the worship band in order to help others worship through the sound of the mix. But have you ever thought about what it is that we're really doing beneath the surface?

I used to not think about it much. I just thought it was a cool thing I got to do every once in a while. It was technical and I enjoyed that. It was good fun and I got to worship while doing it, but I know I've certainly gone through the motions in worship, in the midst of the body and especially behind the board. We check out, we're on social media, thinking about lunch, trying to find our friends in the crowd; we're bored and distracted. We've forgotten who we are and we think we're only doing a job, a job that somebody just has to do.

It's time to wake up.

The reality? We're serving and worshiping a Holy God. A God who should be wholly feared and desperately loved! If we were to see beyond the veil of this world to who it is we are worshiping, this Holy, Living God, it would terrify us to the core and cause us to cry out like Isaiah.

> And I said: "Woe is me! For I am lost; for I am a man of unclean lips, and I dwell in the midst of a people of unclean lips; for my eyes have seen the King, the Lord of hosts!" (Isa. 6:5)

I remember when I first read Francis Chan's book, *Crazy Love*. In the first chapter, the first paragraph even, Chan encourages the reader to "stop praying" and consider simply looking at God before even speaking. He talks of the warning Solomon gives about rushing into the presence of God.

> Guard your steps when you go to the house of God. To draw near to listen is better than to offer the sacrifice of fools, for they do not know that they are doing evil. 2 [b] Be not rash with your mouth, nor let your heart be hasty to utter a word before God, for God is in heaven and you are on earth. Therefore let your words be few. (Ecc. 5:1-2)

I don't think I picked up the book for a solid week after reading that. It stopped me right in my tracks. It made me question everything I had been doing as a sound engineer up to that point. How careless, and at times reckless, I had been in considering what it is that I'm doing with worship. I pray that Solomon's warning resonates with you as it did me. Even the seraphim have to cover their eyes while in His presence as they cry out day and night,

> "Holy, Holy, Holy is the Lord of hosts;
>   the whole earth is full of His glory." (Isa. 6:3)

Only in Christ can we safely look out into the storm that is God's holiness—an infinitely powerful, wholly righteous, and terrifying beauty that only draws us closer and causes us to gasp in awe at its nature.

> Worship is a mixture of fear and joy, awe and intimacy, terror and celebration; it isn't total terror nor is it total elation.
>   —Matt Papa

Whether we realize it or not, we are partnered with the worship leader to create something beautiful, to worship this Holy God. Something that draws our eyes high above and beyond ourselves, that touches the soul and plucks on the heartstrings of humanity: the mixing of musical instruments and voices in such a way that it points to the fount of beauty, God Himself. And the purpose? If only to catch a glimpse of God's holiness, His glory. For in that moment, we worship this Holy God because we see a greater glory than anything in this world. And we are forever changed by it.

You may consider yourself "just a sound person." You may have years of experience or maybe you only do it because no one else can. But do you realize that you too can create something beautiful? That you are a part of a collaboration of worshiping artists working to create something beautiful? Not just emotion, but beauty. Man is made to worship, made for God's glory; our hearts yearn for beauty and perfection.

Only in Christ can our hearts be truly satisfied and our eyes filled with the beauty of God.[1] Because when we catch a glimpse of His glory, the true beauty, the truth of the gospel changes us, shapes us, and resonates throughout every aspect of our lives.

More than just a sound engineer, but a worshiper—that's who we are. It is our task to serve and worship with the body by lifting our eyes to see something, or better yet, hear something beautiful so that we might gain a larger vision of Jesus. And in a perfect world, every Sunday would be beautiful; every mix would be perfect, and every heart in the room would be worshiping this Holy God.

But the flesh hates worship, because when we worship we declare that something is more important than ourselves. Worship is a selfless giving and outpouring of the heart. The flesh wants to be affirmed, it wants to be recognized, it wants the best for itself, and perhaps, in a sound engineer's case, it wants to be heard. Serving in sound, we don't receive much affirmation in what we do, and it doesn't take the flesh long to redirect the attention to itself.

It happens subtly at first, then only growing in boldness. It's like being the best man at a wedding and trying to get the bride's attention off the groom as she walks down the aisle, waving our hands in the air and flexing our muscles as if to say, "Hey look at me! I'm pretty great too!"

And I've been that guy, well… I mean not the actual best man bit. But I have certainly tried to make worship all about me. And for a long time I didn't even realize I was doing it. It wasn't until I truly began to let the seeds of the gospel penetrate my heart that I began seeing what worship really looks like. It's more than actions, more than words; it's about the heart and what's coming out of it.

Sound in the Gospel was written from a growing desire to see church sound engineers (or any worship/tech person) develop a gospel mindset alongside their technical skills. The pressures put on them are tremendous and can result in the most quickly burned out volunteer positions in the church. With little support, relief, affirmation, or encouragement, they are asked, more often than not, to fill the position every single Sunday.

Having a technical understanding simply isn't enough. Their interaction with the body sets a tone for the worship team, pastors, and other volunteers. This one position can become a cancer to the entire body if negativity goes unchecked. Technical and musical knowledge MUST be paired with a gospel mentality if anything is going to change. And it all starts in one place…

---

[1] Gen. 2:16; Isa. 43:7; 1 Cor. 10:31; Matt. 4:1; Psa. 84:2, 27:4

Part I
Sound in the Gospel

Chapter One

It's All About GAIN

So, there was this time I almost got thrown off of a balcony by a lighting volunteer. I was working as a sound engineer for a church while also working for a production company. We had just had a really late load-out for a big production the night before, and I was out-of-my-mind tired. I was at a point with the church where I really didn't want to be there anymore. I felt underpaid, under-appreciated and overlooked. Anything I could think of to whine about, I probably did. And that particular Sunday, it was really bad.

What actually happened that day is a bit of a blur, but I remember the band was being exceptionally needy, and perhaps rightly so, but I moaned and groaned about it. And the lighting guy wasn't running lights like he was supposed to (or rather, as I thought he should). I don't completely recall the conversation that followed, but it ended with my back to the balcony and a large Mexican man threatening to throw me over the rail. I remember thinking, "I'm really about to get into a physical fight at church," and if I'm being honest, "This is it, this is how I end."

This same Sunday a little old lady came back during the service and literally screamed at me about how loud it was. I told her that she should just go worship outside of the building. Yeah, that Sunday was a real winner for me on a personal level.

I did finally come to terms with the lighting volunteer and the little old lady, after eating a fair share of humble pie. I look back at that Sunday with a lot of embarrassment and shame, but also with thankfulness for God's grace and patience with me. I've grown a lot since then, but there are still days I probably deserve to be thrown off the balcony.

The Flesh vs. The Spirit

There's an old story that I feel really resonates with the struggle between the flesh and the spirit.

> A grandfather was talking to his grandson about how he felt. He said, "I feel as if I have two wolves fighting in my heart… One wolf is the vengeful, angry, violent one. The other wolf is the loving, compassionate one." The grandson asked him, "Which wolf will win the fight?" The grandfather answered, "The one I feed."

So let's talk about the spirit vs. the flesh in our world as sound engineers. Which one do we feed the most? I confess, as I sit here and write this, I'm thinking of my own attitude on that terrible Sunday (and on a few others). I know I don't meet every request with gladness. Instead of responding with respect and love to that elderly lady who forcefully informed me that the music was too loud (like she does every Sunday), I lost my temper.

Does it frustrate me to give the bass player more bass in his monitor (after he's asked five different times) or do I patiently ask what else I can do for him? I might be more concerned with refilling my cup of coffee than meeting his needs. I struggle to keep my cool when a volunteer forgets to change the batteries in the pastor's mic…AGAIN. I don't always keep my thoughts to myself about the worship set or a background singer's pitchy vocals, which encourages everyone at front of house (or FOH) to think negatively too.

Our Influence Over the Body

Even if I kind of check out while mixing, as long as every-thing sounds fine, then no one necessarily knows that my heart is elsewhere. Am I representing the gospel, or am I just being profes-sional so I can keep my position? Did I actually do anything that might help further the Kingdom of God while I served at FOH last Sunday? I certainly fail in some of these areas. And maybe you do as well.

Have you ever stopped to consider how much power and influence you can have over the body as a sound engineer? Our actions and words are an overflow of our hearts. The tongue is far more damaging to the body of Christ than the faders we push. The sound engineer actually interacts with a lot of people other than the band—volunteers, other techs, elders, staff, guests, the congre-gation, and most importantly, pastors.

Have you thought about the impact you have on the presen-tation of the gospel? You need to realize that you are in charge of making sure the most important message of all time is heard and understood, clearly. You can distract people, or worse, prevent them from hearing the gospel if something is wrong, such as feedback, buzzing, or muted mics.

And remember that you're not the only one that gets crit-icized. Pastors are often intercepted before going on stage to preach. They have to listen to complaints about this and that, often about how the sound isn't quite up to someone's standards. Can you imagine for a moment how that must pull his head out of the game right before he preaches? Not only does he have to deal with the stressful situation of the complainer, but it also throws in possible insecurities about how he will sound from the pulpit. "Will the sound be ok? Will there be feedback? Will my mic even be turned on?"

We can eliminate these insecurities not only by doing our job correctly, but also by crucifying our flesh in light of our respon-sibility to the gospel as it relates to the job. Can the Holy Spirit operate without a sound system and communicate no matter how it sounds? Of course! But consider this,

25

And how are they to believe in Him of whom they have never heard? And how are they to hear without someone preaching? And how are they to preach unless they are sent? As it is written, "HOW BEAUTIFUL ARE THE FEET OF THOSE WHO PREACH THE GOOD NEWS!" (Rom. 10:14-15, emphasis added)

Jesus spoke without a sound system to thousands on a mount next to the Sea of Galilee, and this same Jesus is using you to help proclaim His gospel to hundreds, or maybe even thousands, each Sunday. Now, this next bit may be a little silly, but stay with me. Take off your shoes and look at your feet. Because according to Romans 10:15, they're beautiful. Every time you step into FOH and push up the fader for the pastor, you are partnering with him in the gospel, and this gospel is too important for us not to regularly consider how it's being communicated from the pulpit, FOH, and our own hearts.

I know it may seem like I'm being pretty hard on the average church sound volunteer, but I feel that among our ranks there is a major layer of apathy surrounding this topic. In particular, we tend to feel that nothing is ever going to change. That hopelessness is felt by far too many and the gospel is the only thing that can penetrate it. So, we have to bring the darkness to light and face our own flesh. As Pastor Danny Franks of the Summit Church often reminds the congregation, "Entitlement kills the body."

It Really is All About GAIN.

If I could tell you just one thing about sound, it would be that "it's all about GAIN." Gain structure is the foundation of every sound system and every mix. It's going to affect every frequency, determine how you handle almost any situation that might arise, and will be the place you go back to when there's a problem. It's going to affect every channel on your board. And not only will it affect your mix at FOH, it will even affect what's happening on stage. If your gain foundation is not set up correctly, there will be feedback. You won't be able to mix properly and there will be... (dun, dun, dun...) complaints.

While I'm certainly not trying to over-spiritualize this, it is interesting that there is a direct correlation in scripture that mirrors setting gain structure to the condition of our own hearts. Because if our hearts are not set properly in the gospel, if we are not walking in step with the Spirit, our lives will become a big noisy mess. When problems arise, they won't be met with a loving response. Love, at this point, becomes a rarity because the works of the flesh come fully to bear on the body (1 Cor. 13).

Let's look to one scripture to see the ways the desires of the flesh can affect the body.

> But I say, walk by the Spirit, and you will not gratify the desires of the flesh. For the desires of the flesh are against the Spirit and the desires of the Spirit are against the flesh, for these are opposed to each other, to keep you from doing the things you want to do. But if you are led by the Spirit you are not under the law. Now the works of the flesh are evident:…idolatry… enmity, strife, jealousy, fits of anger, rivalries, dissensions, divisions, envy…and things like these. I warn you, as I warned you before, that those who do such things will not inherit the kingdom of God." (Gal. 5:16-21)

Did anything stand out to you? I know that I can quickly identify many of those as sins I've committed—a lot of them while working/serving as a sound engineer! This list is straight from scripture and it's interesting that it so quickly and accurately describes common attitudes seen in a church sound person. Also look at the warning in verse 21. Whose kingdom are you really serving: the Kingdom of God, or the Kingdom of Me?

Read it again. Maybe you should take a moment before reading further to talk with God, to pray and repent over the works of your flesh.

Where we set our hearts is just as important as how technically and proficiently we run our gigs. That's why gain is so important. It sets a firm foundation for us to work from. The same goes for the heart—our personal foundation—and where we put our trust.

We need to remind ourselves where our foundation is every time we step into FOH to mix and serve the body.

> Christ Jesus Himself being the cornerstone, in whom the whole structure, being joined together, grows into a holy temple in the Lord. (Eph. 2:20-21)

With all the authority and power Jesus had within Himself, as the foundation of the church He chose to make Himself a servant, obedient even unto death. This is the perfect example of laying down our rights, an example Christ points us to daily. Daily servant-hearted devotion.

The Kingdom of Me

So how are we doing? Are we laying down our rights as sound engineers? Or are we building up the walls of the Kingdom of Me? I realize these truths are probably Sunday School fundamentals for many Christians, but the problem for most of us is that we've started the gospel in the wrong place. We start with "Jesus Loves Me" or "Jesus Loves You," and while these statements are entirely true, it's far too easy to incorrectly highlight whom the gospel is about. And whether we subconsciously or consciously do this, we end up making the gospel about "me," which the flesh loves.

The gospel needs to begin with "God is holy." When we start the gospel with God's holiness, our hearts submit to the reality that God is infinitely powerful, righteous, and justified, and that we are irreparably sinful. This perspective change begins to break up the foundations of the Kingdom of Me. Only then can we truly begin to deny our flesh and take up our crosses. As sound engineers, this is where we must begin to reset the gain structure of our hearts. Let's read how Paul communicated this terrible yet beautiful truth.

> And you were dead in the trespasses and sins in which you once walked, following the course of this world, following the prince of the power of the air, the spirit that is now at work in the sons of disobedience—

among whom we all once lived in the passions of our flesh, carrying out the desires of the body and the mind, and were by nature children of wrath, like the rest of mankind. But God, being rich in mercy, because of the great love with which He loved us, even when we were dead in our trespasses, made us alive together with Christ—by grace you have been saved. (Eph. 2:1-5)

Please don't skip over this scripture just because we've all read it before. Take a breath and read it again, giving your eyes enough time to adjust to the desperation of our situation and the glorious pursuit of Christ.

The Works of the Flesh

To begin resetting our hearts, we need to open our eyes to what end the flesh can truly bring. Every time we walk into the sound booth we go to battle with our flesh. It wants to be recognized and heard. When you start as a new church volunteer, you may be okay with not being acknowledged. You might receive some compliments on your mix the first couple of Sundays. You might have a few conflicts with the worship leader or with scheduling that need to be worked out.

But things settle in and eventually you reach a point where it becomes automatic. It's assumed that you're the guy that's going to make things happen. The compliments and thanks slowly fade away. Then the complaints come, some from a distance and some right to your face. More conflicts arise, and you're beginning to get tired, so you bend to the will of the Church. You're just trying to serve, right?

At some point (you may even remember the Sunday it happened) you become invisible. Well that's part of the job, right? You're just in the back, making things happen. But then, you start to get lazy, sloppy, late. This causes more conflict. Things between you and the band begin to get tense. A wall goes up between FOH and the stage. You feel the pressure when things aren't perfect, you're told your mixes aren't good enough. Then something terrible happens: you begin to justify the stress you feel. You begin to believe certain things don't apply to you anymore because you have to deal with so much.

You just make decisions, trying to survive. Then the day arrives that the church leadership recognizes you. (At last!) You are put in charge of the entire sound system: all the mics, amps, speakers, and digital signal processors you can manage. And if anyone wants to change anything they have to go through you. It's your baby now. And your flesh loves the power behind that.

Your complaints are no longer kept only to yourself, but are blabbed to anyone who cares to listen. And they can't help but agree with you, because you've defended yourself so well. You feel even more justified and get bolder in your opinions, because they're the only ones that matter now. The flesh absolutely loves it. You're the person that makes things happen right?

What used to be passive aggressive mumbles keep growing and when the right moment presents itself, you let loose, swinging at anything. You're living on instinct and at the whim of the flesh.

You're exhausted, hungry, thirsty, and you're hurting yourself and those around you. You're locked in; you're stuck. There isn't anyone else that can do what you do. You don't want it to be this way, but you feel you have no choice. You feel alone. You've isolated yourself from the body and before you know it, you've helped create an atmosphere in the body. But it's not of the Spirit, it's of the flesh. How did you even get here? All you wanted to do was serve the body, and now you just despise it.

For some of you, maybe this has absolutely outlined your experience. If it has, I am so sorry. I have walked a path much like this and it is exhausting and terrible. Likely for most of you, there are bits and pieces you identify with.

I know there are those of you out there that simply haven't let this happen! You've walked with grace, patience, and love and you're still mixing and running the race well! And that's amazing, so keep going! Praise God! But don't check out on me just yet. Because we can all identify with parts of this story even if it is the hypothetical "for all have sinned and fall short of the glory of God" (Rom. 3:23).

To those of you who've never thought about how your actions reflect your heart, or pieced together how the gospel meets the technical: understand that you can have all the technical knowledge in the world or years of musical experience, but if you have not love, it counts for nothing. You're just making noise (1 Cor. 13). So how in the world are we supposed to do this, in light of all of our stress and pressure? What does it look like to walk in the Spirit while we're serving the body through sound?

The Fruit of the Spirit

> But the fruit of the Spirit is love, joy, peace, patience, kindness, goodness, faithfulness, gentleness, self-control; against such things there is no law. (Gal. 5:22-23)

This is the standard we are called to as followers of Christ. It would be amazing if we walked out each of these traits every Sunday! Remember the works of the flesh quoted at the beginning of the chapter? Consider the contrast in how Paul labels the "*fruit* of the Spirit." It isn't "*works* of the Spirit." We can't just pull up our bootstraps and produce them. They come as a result of the Spirit working in us, of having new desires within us that are greater than what our flesh desires (2 Cor. 5:17). And we must consider and reconsider—every single day—that we are new creatures in Christ.

Now, I don't know where you're at in your walk with Christ, and all this stuff may be tough to swallow. As believers we all know that the standard for any Christian to follow is Christ, but what we often forget is that this also includes His suffering. The standard doesn't change for us simply because things get tough while serving the Church. There is no opting out. There is no room for our fleshly desires when worshiping this Holy God.

We have to know our place not only as sound engineers, but as human beings. As sound engineers we should be the most humble part of the body because of the scope of influence we can have over worship and the gospel. We must take up our crosses and proclaim with our tongues and our hearts that Jesus is Lord. Daily.

As my friend and fellow sound engineer Brian Self says, "If youwant to follow Christ, and especially if you want to run sound at church, it requires you to be 100% humble."

Run Away!

So at this point, you may want to take Paul Rice's advice and run away! (Which, frankly, I can understand. I've wanted to at times!) Being a sound engineer isn't for the faint of heart. But if you're like me, you know the mission is great, the cost will be much, and the reward of Christ is even greater.

Maybe you really struggle to know how to walk out the gospel in your own life, let alone as a sound engineer! We know that we are called to walk in step with the Spirit. But with our flesh getting in the way, how are we supposed to do this? We have to have a firm foundation. Because when the overflow of the heart is of the flesh, it's typically rooted in some form of insecurity. For a lot of sound engineers, that insecurity falls into one of two camps: You're either...

"In Over Your Head" or "The Know-It All"

Chapter Two

In Over Your Head &
The Know-It-All

In Over My Head

I can still remember the first time I stepped into the FOH booth with Paul. The sound board seemed so massive to me back then—so many knobs, labels, and lights. I remember thinking to myself, "I'll never learn what each of these knobs do." But Paul patiently and humorously explained each section of the board, showing me the gain knob, the EQ knobs, aux knobs, the "Suck" knob and even a button that releases the hounds! Then he took me over to the master fader, a fader that was labeled "Gas!" He said to me, "And this is where you go if you need to give your mix more Gas!" Paul was funny that way.

Things were very new back then, and I tried to absorb every bit of it that I could. I would sit to the left of Paul for the coming months as I "helped" him mix the chapel services and numerous events that came through the halls of KCC. Paul had me manage channels 1-8 on the SoundCraft Spirit II and he would handle the rest. (These were the drum channels, and in hindsight it was probably pretty dangerous that Paul let me manage them!) I would learn about how to set gain structure, how to plug everything in, how to

EQ, how to mix, and especially how to roll cables! I had a really great teacher who was able to work with me one on one. If I had a question, Paul would have an answer, most of the time that answer being "42." (If you don't know what this means, then please read *The Hitchhiker's Guide to the Galaxy*.) (Or read it anyways.) (Did I mention that Paul was a geek?) (Did I mention that I am a geek?)

When my time with Paul was done, he sent me on some gigs with his local friends. I would try a few things on my own, but I mostly just did as I was told. I was still learning, but somewhere along the way I reached a point where I felt I had a general idea of what I was doing. Now I wasn't a good sound tech, I was basically just dangerous with my knowledge. I had just enough that I could hurt people, sonically and also relationally. Deep down I knew that I didn't yet have the experience or skills to be completely confident as an engineer, but I didn't want anyone to know that.

I remember whenever a musician would come in that knew less about production or sound than I did, I was more than glad to inform him or her that I knew exactly what I was doing. It didn't always come across as arrogantly as that, but it wasn't helpful either. My ego just wanted them to recognize my abilities and the stress or the pressure I felt from the event would dictate how I treated them. I could be helpful or careless with my words, and a lot of times I would be so stressed out that I wouldn't care which. I was a believer at the time and I was trying to follow Christ in my daily life, but with this new knowledge, one that a lot of people knew nothing about, a seed of pride was planted deep in my heart.

I began working for secular production companies and larger events in the area, as well as with some very experienced sound techs. Paul told me before I started, "If you wanna work these bigger gigs then you're gonna need to have some thick skin." Boy was he right. The old saying, "crap rolls down hill" is especially true when it comes to the world of production.

As the new guy I got yelled at, cursed at, and talked about behind my back. Some of it was just from being new and some of it was because there was a lot that I didn't know. At times I wouldn't ask for help, because I wanted to show them I could figure stuff out. And man, I got a lot wrong back in those days.

I remember my heart struggling to rest in a place of contentment, which kept me from taking criticism. If I messed up or let down a senior sound tech, it would destroy me on the inside. Not only would I do my job more poorly, but my flesh would start trying to justify itself in any way it could. Sometimes I would take it out on someone else, someone not connected with the production, or someone that deep down, I felt I was better than.

So what was my problem? That I didn't know enough and needed to learn more? That I just needed to have a more humble attitude? That I needed to admit that I needed help? That I just needed to man up and deal with stress better? Yes. But there was a deeper need that wasn't being satisfied, and it was affecting every aspect of my life, a need which I'll come back to later.

I Knew It All

Fast-forward about five or six years to when I became a little more seasoned. I could bring up a mix fairly quickly and take care of the band at the same time. By this point I had worked for several production companies, churches, and a handful of touring artists. I was beginning to be respected and trusted as a sound tech. But if I walked into a situation where things weren't quite right or not as I had asked for on the band rider, I was sure to correct them and point out why it was wrong. Much like before, the stress of the day would entirely dictate how I treated someone who made a mistake, whether it was a trainee, musician, or just a volunteer.

If someone asked me a question I didn't know much about, I would make excuses or change the question so you wouldn't know that I didn't have an answer. I couldn't just say, "That's a good question, I really don't know." I might have responded instead with, "It's really not that important."

I was a "professional," so if someone asked a stupid question, they got a stupid answer. If someone challenged the way I did something, even if they wanted to learn, a quiet pride would burn through my heart. And God forbid, if someone came back and said, "Gee, what do all these knobs do?" My glare could have cut them in half. "What does that one do? ...It explodes the worship leader..."

Humility was not my first response to anything. My experience as a professional sound engineer blinded me to the comments and opinions of others. If someone, even a person in authority, came back and told me something didn't sound right and I didn't agree, I'd do the old "I'm turning knobs to fix it, but not really" trick to get them to go away. My attitude guided how I handled these situtations.

The Symptoms of a Deeper Problem

As I grew as a sound engineer, I found that the things I struggled with personally seemed to grow too. The problems weren't going away, they were just developing in new ways. Let's break these two groups down a little further and look at some of their traits and symptoms. See if you identify with any of these.

In Over Your Head	The Know-It-All
- Limited to no training	- More experience/training, may have some good skills
- No reference for what sounds good, so he creates his own standards	- Has some secular sound production experience
- More technical than musical	- Is a Sound Veteran (AAA Sound Tech)
- Thinks he's the only one in the body that can do it	- Can be over-opinionated
- Hides areas of production he doesn't understand (territorial)	- Might be a musician
- Responds poorly to being questioned	- Was "in over his head" but is now self-affirmed
- Doesn't handle stress well and lashes out if pushed too far	- Will quickly correct those who know less about sound
- Doesn't try to improve his skill sets	- Struggles to admit errors
- Paralyzed by a lack of knowledge	- Hoards sound system knowledge (territorial)
- Struggles to admit he needs help	- Doesn't train volunteers well
	- May have interpersonal conflicts

So Where is Our Identity?

Sound engineers are typically in one of these two groups, but you may find yourself somewhere in between. As human beings, and especially as sound engineers, we each deal with our own identity issues. At some point we all identify ourselves with our role, position, or job. Because people associate who we are with what we do, we begin to believe that's what gives us worth, which is not scripturally true at all.

People who struggle with this tend to forget a core truth about themselves: they're not just sound engineers, but children of God! The reality is that they have placed their identity in a job and not in their Savior. Then if someone questions them, it challenges that misplaced identity and the fleshly symptoms of this problem are exposed.

Both of these types of sound engineers are almost completely wrapped up with what other people think about them. The guy in over his head is afraid that everyone will find out he doesn't really know what he's doing, and the know-it-all needs everyone to remember and acknowledge that he is a skilled professional. And when our insecurities are exposed or challenged, we see our flesh come to light because we are not rooted in our identity as a child of God.

The flesh tries to justify itself. It tries to reconcile the false identity it's made for itself. But when forced to deal with reality, our flesh starts to thrash about like a child that's been told "no" too many times. Our words, actions, and attitudes are just an overflow of what's in our hearts. (Luke 6:45) The works of the flesh discussed in the first chapter are actually symptoms of this greater problem: something is messing with one of our deeply rooted idols. And for our two groups of sound engineers, this idol is called "The Fear of Man."

The Fear of Man

This idol has been at the center of my heart for far too long. I operated for so many years basing my worth on the words of others. If I received criticism, even helpful criticism, my heart would momentarily panic. I would try to listen, but I struggled to keep my flesh from lashing out and making the situation worse. Then for the minutes, and even hours following, it's all I would think about. I would go over and over the conversation in my mind; trying to justify myself, to make myself feel better about it. Even if I received praise right after the criticism, it wouldn't matter because my idol got knocked off its pedestal. And my heart would weep over it like a child that had his toy taken away.

I can recall a time when Matt Papa walked back to FOH to listen to the kick. He said it sounded "floppy," which it did, but my flesh went into overdrive and a thousand thoughts flew through my head.

"Don't you realize I'm working on it?" "Don't you know what I have to deal with?" "Don't you trust me to fix it?" "You don't think I can do this, do you?" And how did I respond? I snapped out, "I'm working on it!"

Such a small phrase, but it revealed the true landscape of my heart. Matt and I quickly resolved the issue and the kick got to sounding like a kick. But what had happened to me internally?

Matt's words basically thumped my idol on its side. How could such a small thing hurt so much? Why did it even matter? The stress I felt was a key indication of the impact the fear of man had on my life. I'd placed my identity in being a professional sound engineer and not as a child of the Risen King. When that identity was challenged, it hurt like hell.

When we substitute anything for God, that is the definition of an idol. Idols come in all sorts of different shapes and sizes, some that are more noticeable than others and some that are so deeply rooted that we may not even be aware we're holding on to them. The stress that we feel as engineers, or just as humans, can often point to where our hearts really are.

> Worry, fear, sadness, and deep depression are smoke from the fires rising from the altars of our idolatry. Follow the trail of that smoke and you'll see where you have substituted something for God.
> –St. Augustine

The idol of the fear of man, let alone all the other little idols I had imbedded in the soil of my heart, would not allow the fruit of the Spirit to take root in my life. I had some major gardening to do, or rather the Holy Spirit did.

Living Water

When we just try to do "good" things or act the right way, it never lasts, endures, or changes anything. We can't simply choose to do better, because we can't fix ourselves. The power of the Holy Spirit is the only thing that does last. Consider how Jesus describes the Holy Spirit as He talks with the Samaritan woman at the well.

> Jesus said to her, "Everyone who drinks of this water will be thirsty again, but whoever drinks of the water that I will give him will never be thirsty again. The water that I will give him will become in him a spring of water welling up to eternal life." (John 4:13-14)

When our hearts are set in the gospel, and not buried in pointless idols, the living water of the Holy Spirit flows throughout our hearts and only then does the fruit of the Spirit begin to grow and multiply. And this time, the "good" things actually last, endure, and change the hearts of those we encounter. When we walk in step with the Spirit, there are ever-increasing moments when we pour out love and grace only to realize afterward, "Wow, that wasn't me."

> For it is God who works in you, both to will and to work for His good pleasure. (Phil. 2:13)

Whenever we try to do something "good" in the flesh, it eventually just falls flat. Whenever we do something just because we know we should but it's not out of love or from the overflow of the heart, it's like painting a Styrofoam ball red and calling it an apple. It may kind of look like an apple, but once someone hands it to you and you examine it, and especially if you bite into it, you certainly know what it's made of! It's not helpful, sweet, nurturing, or fruitful. It's something that doesn't have the capability to multiply, because it's not the real thing. I can try to fake spiritual fruit and try to be "good." But when things get hard, the fake fruit just doesn't cut it, and my idol is exposed for what it is.

Like Paul says, "Walk by the Spirit, and you will not gratify the desires of the flesh." (Gal. 5:16) If you see a pattern in your life of trying to "do good," but you just can't seem to get it right, this is why. We have to walk in the Spirit.

The Terrible, Yet Wonderful Truth of the Gospel

Let's look at just the very beginning of the gospel, before Jesus came to earth, before the cross, and the resurrection. So brace yourself, because this is about to get pretty dark and bleak: this is where our idols go to die.

The word "gospel" means "good news." It doesn't just communicate to us about the salvation we have in Christ, it communicates who God is, our condition as created beings, and our need for salvation. And what it communicates at first is a terrible reality. Take another look at Ephesians 2:

> And you were dead in the trespasses and sins in which you once walked, following the course of this world, following the prince of the power of the air, the spirit that is now at work in the sons of disobedience among whom we all once lived in the passions of our flesh, carrying out the desires of the body and the mind, and were by nature children of wrath, like the rest of mankind. (vv. 1-3)

Let's stop right there for a second. That was all of us before Christ. And that could have been the end of the story right there, but for our idols to die in our hearts, we have to embrace the most terrible truth that we could know as a human being: the declaration of the gospel is that we are wrecked to the core. We are the worst of the worst and there is nothing good in us outside of Christ. In fact, we're dead.[1] We are sinful, condemned by this holy

God, and He is justified in it.[2] We are going to Hell and there is nothing we can do about it. This is officially the worst possible thing a human being can be told.

It's over.
But there is hope. Great hope.

> But God, being rich in mercy, because of the great love with which He loved us, even when we were dead in our trespasses, made us alive together with Christ— by grace you have been saved—and raised us up with Him and seated us with Him in the heavenly places in Christ Jesus, so that in the coming ages He might show the immeasurable riches of His grace in kindness toward us in Christ Jesus. For by grace you have been saved through faith. And this is not your own doing; it is the gift of God, not a result of works, so that no one may boast. For we are His workmanship, created in Christ Jesus for good works, which God prepared beforehand, that we should walk in them." (vv. 4-10)

Is there any greater thing to hear? We were dead and God loved us! He brought us back from the dead! And then He made us His own and gave us everything in Him?!!! Praise God!

The understanding of this scripture is vital, especially in light of the idol of the fear of man. God, the highest authority, has already said the worst possible thing we could hear. He proclaimed that there wasn't anything we could do to save ourselves, that we were done for and there wasn't any worth in us because of our sins. If we just let that sink in for a moment, it reveals the powerlessness of all our idols.

> If any man thinks ill of you, do not be angry with him,
> for you are worse than he thinks you to be.
> —Charles Spurgeon

Because then and only then do the critical words of other people lose their importance in light of what the gospel has already declared over us! There is nothing anyone on this earth can say that could be worse than what the gospel has proclaimed about us. (Let that sink in for a moment.)

This reality is what roots us in the truth of who we truly are. Because of this, we can stop struggling to try to save ourselves, finally rest in the grace that is ours through the resurrection of Jesus Christ, and lay our idols down! God saved us! He did what we could not! His grace is sufficient no matter what our situation might be.

We can stop letting the critical words of other people destroy our hearts and accept that we are solid with the absolute highest authority there is: the Lord Jesus! Hallelujah! We have been ransomed and adopted into the family of God. Nothing can change that.

Our identity and security is now found in Christ, the struggle to save ourselves is over. It's simply who we are now. Rest in that.

> Your identity is whatever makes you feel the most significant. What makes you feel the most significant is what you put the most weight upon.
>
> –J.D. Greear

[1]Rom. 3:9-20; Col. 2:13
[2]Rom. 5:12, 6:23; Gen. 18:25

Chapter Three

For the Knucklehead Tech in All of Us

The truth and beauty of the gospel is ours everyday, so long as we keep our eye on the prize: Jesus (Heb. 12:2). But, I may wake up the very next morning and forget this. I get up late, forget to eat breakfast, rush into the church, hastily patch in the band, and make mistakes. I get stressed and start to worry, looking around for who might be watching me, and that idol of the fear of man stands right back up in my heart.

We can have head knowledge about the gospel, even understand doctrine and theology, but rooting it in our hearts is another thing entirely. Why? Our hearts are distracted, we don't linger, we don't behold. We're not seeing Him. It is a daily battle each of us has to fight. Let's look at some practical ways to help the gospel take root in our hearts. A great place to begin is in Matthew 13.

> And He told them many things in parables, saying: "A sower went out to sow. And as he sowed, some seeds fell along the path, and the birds came and devoured them. Other seeds fell on rocky ground, where they

did not have much soil, and immediately they sprang up, since they had no depth of soil, but when the sun rose they were scorched. And since they had no root, they withered away. Other seeds fell among thorns, and the thorns grew up and choked them. Other seeds fell on good soil and produced grain, some a hundredfold, some sixty, some thirty. He who has ears, let him hear." (vv. 3-9)

How do these verses apply to us as sound engineers? First let's look at the "soil" of our hearts. There are many things that can snatch up, crowd out, and choke the seeds of the gospel. As I grew as a sound engineer and a Christian, I began identifying areas of my life that were triggers for my flesh, things that would throw my old self into overdrive. It could be a previously unidentified idol, a blind spot in my character, or simply lack of trust in God.

Tilling the Soil

Whenever we start to feel in over our heads, there are a few practical things that can help build up confidence before heading to the church. Get up early so you won't feel rushed. Eat a good breakfast because we always think more clearly and carefully on a full stomach (and everyone gets hangry!). Make sure to spend time in the Word, not to check it off your list, but to linger and abide in the Word, to look for the beauty of the Creator and hear what He wants to speak to you.

Once your soul is "happy in the Lord," as my cohort Tim Keeler would say, spend time worshiping and praying as you head to the church. Pray, "God, forgive me of my unbelief. Forgive me for not believing I am who You say I am and that You are who You say You are."

During your time alone in the sanctuary while prepping the stage, pray for the service, the musicians, the pastor, the gospel, or whatever the Spirit puts on your mind. As you prepare, ask for understanding (spiritual and technical), and for help building relationships with the band, pastors, and congregation. This will help to begin a habit of continuous prayer throughout the day, through sound check, the mix, the sermon, and troubleshooting issues. Preparation always helps to reduce stress and also equips us to do our jobs properly.

There are plenty of days I forget to do these things. There are days I even forget what I'm actually there to do: worship! I try to remember that by doing these things, they ground me in my identity in Christ. Things slowly start to settle and I find that the soil of my heart is tilled and ready for the seeds of the gospel.

Earlier in my tech days, it was especially good for me to get in ahead of time, to check all the connections, and learn a little bit about the sound system. There was a time when I didn't understand a thing about patching (and there are still days that the idea of cross-patching makes my brain explode).

Half-Hearted Worship

As I grew in my knowledge and confidence as an engineer, I would find myself less in over my head and more the know-it-all. There would be many mornings that I would come in and half-heartedly do my job. I felt I didn't have to prepare technically. I wouldn't get there early. I would trust in my experience to get the job done. And frankly that was the problem; it was just a "job" to me.

I know that some of you are volunteers and some of you are paid sound engineers (and the discussion of business vs. ministry is probably another whole book in itself). But let me bottom line this: as sound engineers in the church, we have to remember whom we are serving. It's not the pastors, or the staff, or even those who cut our checks. It is a Holy God who takes even half-hearted worship very seriously. Consider what we're offering God when we go through the motions in serving the church. Look at this passage in Malachi when Israel breaks its covenant with the Lord through blemished offerings.

> "A son honors his father, and a servant his master. If then I am a father, where is My honor? And if I am a master, where is My fear? says the Lord of hosts to you, O priests, who despise My name. But you say, 'How

47

have we despised your name?' By offering polluted food upon My altar. But you say, 'How have we polluted you?' By saying that the Lord's table may be despised. When you offer blind animals in sacrifice, is that not evil? And when you offer those that are lame or sick, is that not evil? Present that to your governor; will he accept you or show you favor? says the Lord of hosts. And now entreat the favor of God, that He may be gracious to us. With such a gift from your hand, will He show favor to any of you? says the Lord of hosts. (Mal. 1:6-9)

Working for the church can be a double-edged sword. It's great to receive compensation for our time and skill sets. But it's also a place where the flesh will begin to justify itself as we then begin to base our worth on the size of our paycheck. It feeds our cravings to be perceived as the professional. It causes us to care less about what we're offering the Lord. It makes us feel "compensated" for our sacrifice of worship.

The thing is, all of our sacrifices are insufficient. Our best mix, singing, serving, or giving will never be enough. Only Christ's perfect sacrifice is truly sufficient. And when we rest in God's acceptance of our offerings, the heart behind our work can become motivated by our gratitude for God's acceptance and grace.

I know I've struggled with this, and the apathy that results can allow me to fake my way through the job. I could easily get my mix in the ballpark and then not even pay much attention to have a "successful service." Instead of using my time in the booth for prayer or worship, I would make little idols out of my precious system settings, EQ, reverbs, delay throws, and compression rates. I would mix to satisfy my own preference and post my latest sound discoveries on social media. I would be glad to show off to whoever stepped into the booth, but I wouldn't dare let anyone change anything.

I even got in the habit of recording my mixes, at first for my own improvement and enjoyment, but as my mixes got better I made sure people heard the recordings after service or burned a CD for who ever would ask for one. Such a pitiful, silly idol. I wasn't worshiping God; I was worshiping myself! I was standing in the way of God being glorified. And this idol wasn't even satisfying; in fact it was drying me up on the inside.

Made to Worship

In my time working with Matt Papa I've heard him talk a lot about how we are made to worship.

> When we cease to worship God, we do not worship nothing. We worship anything.
> –G. K. Chesterton

And it's so true. At his shows, Matt often asks, "What are you looking at?" What we're looking at is often what we're worshiping. It's what we talk about the most, what we think about when we're alone, where our time is freely spent and even where our money effortlessly flows. I've heard Matt say these things many times over the course of many events. It makes me ask, "What am I looking at?"

Through the lens of a sound engineer, I began to see the answer. Not only was I concerned with how I was perceived, but also with my skill level. How quickly these things began diverting my eyes off of Jesus. The point of what we do as sound engineers, the point of everything we do, is worship. And I was worshiping everything but Jesus.

So I began questioning what it was that I was thinking and talking about the most. It didn't take long to see that I didn't love Jesus nearly half as much as I thought I did! I was consumed with all sorts of things—some good, some not so good, and some really bad—that ultimately reflected what it was in my heart that I really loved, even more than Jesus. So I challenge you with this question in light of what we do as sound engineers:

What is it that you're looking at?

Take some time to pray about this and take a break from the book if you need to.

49

Just Stop

When was the last time you stopped what you were doing in the sound booth and looked out at everything that was happening in the room? Just stopped and looked? Consider the musicians on the stage, the talent that God placed in each of them, the strength and courage God brought out of them to stand on the stage and praise His name. Think about the story of each person, what God has brought them through. Linger on the grand piano, the brilliance behind the design of it. God inspired a human mind to dream, design, and create a device that has all these moving parts that need to be constantly cared for and tuned. So many things have to work correctly for it function. And when it does: beauty.

Consider the human voice, the wonder of the design of it: air flowing over the muscles to shape the sound that comes out, a unique sound to each and every person. Ponder the bizarre nature of the banjo, the soothing sounds of a brilliantly played violin.

Think about the microphone: air waves being transformed into electrical impulses that travel down a cable to a pre-amp that flows through a sound board that boosts and cuts the individual frequencies of the sound wave. Then it gets pushed back down the cable to an amp which amplifies the signal into a speaker and is transformed BACK into moving air. It's baffling when you really think about it (especially if you didn't understand any of that). And it's amazing. We may be inclined to give credit to the performers or inventors.

We look for what we can understand, what we can relate to, what gives us instant satisfaction, and ultimately what we can control. It's easier to behold that glory. Beholding the glory of God is more difficult. What we need to say is, "Wow! God is such an amazing, beautiful creator whose creativity knows no bounds! And I belong to HIM." We have to go back to looking at the world in wonder, like a child, (Matt. 18:3) feasting our eyes on the glorious nature of creation.

We've forgotten how to behold, how to linger, and to savor the goodness of God. We're often hindered by our lack of attention, our inability to fully comprehend with human minds. We catch a glimpse, but we have to look away. It's too bright, too much. When Moses asked to see the glory of the Lord, he could only be shown His back. Moses' face shone so brightly afterwards, that he had to cover it with a veil.[1]

Matt Papa is fond of saying, "We have to let our eyes adjust." The glory of God is overwhelming. We have to linger until this glory overtakes us.

It's what we were made to do! It's what allows us to grow in step with the Spirit. It grows the fruit of the Spirit within us as it transforms us daily into the image of Christ. This is where we begin to see and behold true glory, God's all-surpassing glory. As John Piper says,

> "Christ is the glory of God. His blood-soaked cross is
> the blazing center of that glory."

Now the beauty of the parable in Matthew 14 comes full circle. Here the soil of our hearts must be cleared of seed-choking idols. We must walk in step with the Holy Spirit by dwelling with Him in prayer, which brings living water to our lives. And our eyes must behold the glory of God, the true glory that feeds our heart's desire for worship, a glory that shines on the seeds of the gospel that grows the fruit of the Spirit that multiplies and transforms us. Daily.

Behold it.
Cherish it.
Look and Live.

Note: Much of the content of this chapter is paraphrased from Matt Papa's book *Look and Live*.

[1] Ex. 33:18-23, 34:29-33

Chapter Four

Your Old Nemeses...

The Authority

Custom Audio and Lighting had just finished up an installation at New Covenant Church in Greenwood, South Carolina. I had previously worked with their installation team and I also attended church there. I got to mix that first Sunday on a brand-spanking-new Yorkville Sound System. I had spent time tuning the system and tweaking the monitor wedges to (what I thought was) perfection. Everything was where I wanted it and it was going great until one Sunday when I walked in and it had all changed.

Pastor David Harrell, who at the time doubled as the worship leader, had come in the night before and added some vocal mics, instruments, and more monitor wedges (for which I did not have graphic EQ's and I think he even bypassed some of the graphic EQ's for the ones that I did have!)

Now, I don't remember everything that had actually been changed, but I do remember feeling that all my hard work was gone and that I had been entirely disrespected. I mean, he didn't tell me he was adding a ton more vocalists and instruments. I needed to be notified! He needed to run it by me first, right?

That Sunday, my flesh erupted. I wasn't good for anyone to be around. My idol had gotten knocked on it side and it was resonating throughout the core of my being. I remember communicating my frustration with Pastor Harrell, in a fairly passive aggressive fashion, and we agreed to talk about it later.

We met in his office and he frankly gave me some tough love that has stuck with me to this day. He told me, "Sometimes you need to be willing to look bad on a professional level so that the ministry can go forward."

This struck right to the center of my frustration. I was stressed because all the last minute additions were going to make me look unprepared and unprofessional. I would have to rush to get everything ready. There might be feedback and things may not sound right. I was so concerned with what everyone else thought about me and my mix, I had forgotten I was there to worship.

Submitting to Authority

Now, I could submit to authority if I needed to, but if I thought I was right and if the person in authority had a different opinion (and if I didn't fully respect them at the time), oh man... it was all I could do to keep my flesh from putting them in their "place."

I could have argued with Pastor Harrell about all the reasons it was wrong to bring equipment in at the last minute, and how it would hurt the (precious) production and (my) sound quality. But ultimately Pastor Harrell was the authority God had placed over me, and God calls us to submit to that authority.

> Be subject for the Lord's sake to every human institution, whether it be to the emperor as supreme, or to governors as sent by Him to punish those who do evil and to praise those who do good. For this is the will of God, that by doing good you should put to silence the ignorance of foolish people. Live as people who are free, not using your freedom as a cover-up for evil, but living as servants of God. Honor everyone. Love the brotherhood. Fear God. Honor the emperor. (1 Pet. 2:13-17)

The heart of these verses is that we are to submit to the Lord our Father, who placed authorities over us; trusting in Him, trusting that He knows what's best. And while there are grounds for rejecting authorities that go against the word of God, the point is to submit to all authority, so that others may see it as a submission to an even higher authority. Jesus gives us an example of this while praying in the garden of Gethsemane.

> And going a little farther, He fell on the ground and prayed that, if it were possible, the hour might pass from Him. And He said, "Abba, Father, all things are possible for You. Remove this cup from Me. Yet not what I will, but what You will." (Mark 14:35-36)

Jesus is asking for another way, any way other than the excruciating cross, but we see Jesus humbly submit to His authority, His Father. He does this three different times in this chapter (Mark 14), in the same pattern, and Jesus doesn't repeat himself without a reason; it's usually to get our attention. He's trying to teach us something here.

I know some of you are thinking, "Dude, you have no idea how crazy my worship leader is. You have no idea what he/she puts me through every Sunday." And frankly, I get it. There are some exasperating worship leaders out there. But consider this: how does a leader become a better leader? They have to make mistakes and then learn from those mistakes. (Sometimes it takes a lot of them!) However, mistakes don't justify a lack of submission to the authority they have over us.

The Armor Bearer

There is a way for us to come around our leaders to help them become better leaders. We can act as the armor bearers that we read about in the Old Testament. An armor bearer was typically someone of low status who was assigned as a personal servant to a soldier, typically a commanding officer. The duties of the armor bearer included holding and equipping weapons and armor, following the commander into battle and protecting his rear flank, finishing off enemies that the commander had wounded, and lastly, laying down their lives for their commanders. Their purpose was to help the commander be the best they could be.

If you have a Bible nearby, take a moment to read 1 Samuel 14:1-14, the story of Jonathan and his armor bearer. Jonathan felt that God had handed the Philistines over to them. So without his father's command, Jonathan and his armor bearer set out to fight the entire Philistine army by themselves! Jonathan believed that God was with them (and He was). Can you imagine being that armor bearer? Following your commanding officer into a pretty much guaranteed blood bath? How would you have responded? I know I would have been like, "I don't know about this Jonathan..." But here's how Jonathan's armor bearer responded.

> And his armor-bearer said to him, "Do all that is in your heart. Do as you wish. Behold, I am with you heart and soul. (1 Sam. 14:7)

This sense of honor is a bit lost in our culture. But what can we take away from this? What can we do when we disagree with our "commanding officer?" Let's take a look back at what Jesus shows us in the Garden of Gethsemane. Reread Mark 14:35-36 and look at how it can be broken down into these four actions in this particular order: Pray, Acknowledge, Request and Submit.

> And going a little farther, He fell on the ground and prayed that, if it were possible, the hour might pass from Him. And He said, "Abba, Father, all things are possible for You. Remove this cup from Me. Yet not what I will, but what You will." (Mark 14:35-36)

Pray

The first thing we see Jesus do when He interacts with His authority is pray. When we encounter a potentially bad situation with our leadership, our first response is probably to point out the problem or yell our opinion from FOH. While honesty and directness could be appreciated in some instances, the best possible reaction is to pray before we jump into the heat of a situation—a situation that might involve more than we realize.

When we pray, we submit our flesh to the authority of our Father and ask Him what needs to be said, if anything. There can be a lot of wisdom in not saying anything at all in the moment. Ask the Holy Spirit to guide your next steps. Be patient, pray, take a breath and speak into the situation if prompted by the Spirit.

Acknowledge

The next thing Jesus does is acknowledge the authority put over Him. He addresses God as "Abba Father" and declares God's power, "Everything is possible for You." Now, I'm not saying that when we have a problem with our worship leaders, we should walk up and extol all of their attributes and praise their great works. We can, however, acknowledge that as leaders they make the final decisions and that you want to help. But we can only do this if we've already submitted ourselves in prayer, humbly and honestly, approaching the situation like an armor bearer.

Request

After He verbally recognizes God's authority, Jesus presents His request, "Take this cup from Me." He's pretty direct, succinct, and honest. Because He's already submitted Himself through prayer and acknowledgement, the relationship has stayed intact and His directness will not be interpreted as criticism, but as a request.

When we see that our leadership may be making a mistake, it's as if the commanding officer ran off into battle forgetting a piece of his rear armor. He can't see it, he thinks he's protected, but he's not. We see that it's missing and we want to run after him and try to get his attention so we can equip him properly. Sometimes it's best to wait until after the "battle" to approach problems with leadership. Lovingly try to point out what we thought was missing and how they could correct it for next time. They need to feel respected, so that the relationship with them will to continue to grow.

As I have said, the best way for leaders to become better leaders is to make mistakes. And when they do, it isn't our place to kick them while they're down or talk about them behind their backs, they deserve our respect and we should approach them in private to hand them the missing piece of armor.

Submit

Finally, we see Jesus submit to His Father in the most honest way possible, "Yet not what I will, but what You will." We can offer our leaders their missing pieces of armor, we can try to fix the situation and "finish the job" like the Old Testament armor bearers did, and our commanding officer may run off again without that piece of armor the very next Sunday. All we can do is patiently run after them and start the whole process all over again until they become the leader God has called them to be. The reality is, they might not even listen to us, but what is important is that we submit to the authority of God and trust that God has chosen the right leaders, even though it may seem a bit wacky at the time.

Just to clarify, when I'm talking about this process, I'm speaking mostly about personal issues and production problems. If you find yourself dealing with moral problems, doctrinal issues, or heresy in your leadership, approach the individual privately and then do what is laid out for us in Matthew 18:15-20. Don't try to tackle it on your own and don't let it turn into gossip.

The Complainer

Here we are at last. Our oldest foe: The Complainer. We can see them coming up the aisle from a mile away. You might even get to know them, because they come and tell you what they think every Sunday. I've certainly had my share of little old ladies walking up to the sound booth and verbally eviscerating me, although sometimes they are polite, just unhappy.

Complainers are in every church, and even if the mix is as perfect as we can make it, there will be someone, somewhere that didn't like it. That's just the nature of what we do. Sound is very, very relative sometimes.

So what do we do when we encounter the complainer? I had a conversation with Pastor Matt Moore of Cornerstone Church over coffee one day about this very thing. And he told me something that, to this day, still makes my stomach turn when I think about it. But it's right on.

He said that we should take the complainer to lunch. You mean I should take the time to receive a verbal lashing and deal with all the negativity pouring out of this person? And then love them by taking them out to lunch? Yup. It's the gospel: laying down our rights for someone else, putting someone else's needs ahead of our own. (1 John 3:16)

Invest your time, energy, emotion, and perhaps your sanity for the sake of someone else. We should be more interested in someone else's life than our own. In fact, we should do more than just lunch, coffee, or dinner. We are called to do life together. There is usually something else going on in the complainer's life that is causing all this negativity and pain to come flowing out, and if you take the time to go deep enough you'll usually find what it is. It could be as simple as a need for someone to just listen.

When we talk to complainers amidst the height of tension, we must immediately humanize them. They were created by a Holy God and because of that, they deserve our respect and interest, even if they go a bit overboard. Eugene Peterson says, "People are not problems to be fixed, they are mysteries to be explored."

The more quickly we can get to know these mysteries, and show them that most importantly, they are heard, their guard will drop and they will humanize you. How you react could knock them out of their negative frenzy and bring them back to reality. When we reach out in love and listen to the complainers (and care!), it helps squelch further complaints in the body because they're probably complaining to more people than just you, which could cause division in the body.

When you respond well to your complainer, you may even gain an ally in the body. I've invited some of my complainers to help out with production the next Sunday so that they can feel more a part of what's going on. This might help them gain some perspective on what we do and why things are the way they are.

They could turn out to be helpful critics, and you'll find that they will have a far less hostile attitude toward you because you're no longer just a nameless person running sound.

Even if we fix the sound to make one complainer happy, we would most likely offend someone else or even hurt the mix itself. And there are some people that can't be consoled. You might have to accept the lashing and try not to take it personally. Sometimes the tension we perceive from a complainer and perhaps even the negativity we feel about the person could be the Holy Spirit trying to communicate and convict our own hearts about our own condition.

I used to think it was my responsibility to hand off complainers to the worship leader or the elders, but I was encouraged not to let someone else live out the gospel for me. These are the gospel moments God has handed to you, hard and difficult moments, meant to glorify the Father and transform you into the image of Christ; lean into them.

> Submitting to one another out of reverence for Christ.
> (Eph. 5:21)

Chapter Five

Can't We All Just Get Along?

Partnering with Your Worship Team

Let's shift gears for a moment and talk about our interaction with the worship team as a whole. As part of the production team, we are collaborating artists with the worship leader and musicians. We work with them to paint the biggest picture of Jesus that we can through the worship set.

The apathy that can sometimes surround the sound booth makes us forget that musicians are people too (not just channels on the board!), people with lives and issues, insecurities and baggage. It's important for us to tear down the wall between FOH and the stage, to engage our fellow artists. If we don't, how can we collaborate? Imagine two painters working on the same painting, but at different times and never talking about what the vision actually is!

Have you ever had a conversation with your worship leader about how they want it to sound? They may not have a preference and leave it to you, or they may have a detailed vision but no way of communicating it. They may just tell you to turn the volume up...or, in some cases, down. A few may try to mix from stage if they have a (sometimes understandable) lack of faith in their sound tech, which only makes the situation worse.

This relationship between worship leader and sound engineer is really based on trust, the trust that they will be taken care of and that what they're trying to create will be strengthened through the mix. This trust has to be earned and it also has to be communicated. There needs to be a conversation in which the worship leader casts a vision for the production team. But when navigating potential land mines of miscommunications, conflicts, and differing opinions, it may be hard to have this conversation.

The Power of the Tongue

So where does this conversation start? You. You can start this conversation. This is where you must begin to think like an armor bearer. The worship team has insecurities just as we do. They may feel ill-equipped to be leading the body in worship. But we can come alongside them and encourage them; a kind word can go a long way. Even just letting them know that we will take care of them automatically puts them at ease (ask any musician!).

On the other hand, if we're not careful with our tongues, our careless words will hurt the members of the worship team, which puts their focus on what we said and not on Jesus. We don't know what people are bringing in with them on Sundays. Lives, jobs, marriages, families, children, and relationships could be crumbling behind the veil of a smile. We have to be mindful of this; one thoughtless phrase could destroy someone's spirit and we wouldn't even know.

Some areas of broken trust between the worship team and production team can be found in how we communicate. We know that our tongues can lash out when we're stressed or pushed too far. Passive aggression and complaining can destroy the unity of a worship team, and sarcasm can be a lame excuse for passive aggression.

And while there are some that consider sarcasm an endearing "love language" in a close-knit group, it is important to know the people you work with. We don't always know if someone is going to take what we say the right way. There can be a place for "loving" sarcasm, but we need to make sure we can identify when our teasing or joking around might go too far. I think it best to let our words match what's in our hearts. There's too much at stake in what we're doing.

If we can no longer communicate directly to someone without them having to guess at our true motive and intention, it might be time to reevaluate how we're communicating. Our tongues are a powerful force that can set the atmosphere for worship. Consider what James says about the taming the tongue:

> If we put bits into the mouths of horses so that they obey us, we guide their whole bodies as well. Look at the ships also: though they are so large and are driven by strong winds, they are guided by a very small rudder wherever the will of the pilot directs. So also the tongue is a small member, yet it boasts of great things. How great a forest is set ablaze by such a small fire! And the tongue is a fire, a world of unrighteousness. The tongue is set among our members, staining the whole body, setting on fire the entire course of life, and set on fire by hell. (James 3:3-6)

I've always struggled with bridling my tongue. I've had a lot of thoughts and judgments about people fly through my head throughout the course of a gig. And I've found that my wisest moments were the ones when I kept my mouth shut. There are times when I'd love nothing more than to annihilate someone with my words, to complain about someone behind his back, or just whine about the sound system, band, song choice, or whatever wasn't up to my standards. But here's what actually happens when I give in to these desires of the flesh:

> If I gossip, I both tear down another person and corrupt the mind of my listener. If I complain about the difficult circumstances of my life, I impugn the sovereignty and goodness of God and tempt my listener to do the same.
>
> –Jerry Bridges, *Respectable Sins*

Building up Your Team

When trying to communicate your needs, try to use the old "2 to 1 rule:" give them two compliments to your one criticism. If we come down too hard, it might bring up insecurities and doubts. Of course, each person is coming from a different place and some might react poorly to even the most carefully phrased input. In those cases, it may be helpful to get the worship leader involved, being careful not to slander anybody, but explaining what you need as an engineer. And while we can't control how they respond to what we tell them, we can control how we communicate by making sure our hearts are set in the gospel and our words are said in love. Let's be careful with our words lest we cause someone to take their eyes off of Jesus.

By realizing that worship team members have lives outside of the worship service, we can begin developing and perhaps rebuilding relationships with each of them. It can be as simple as stepping out of FOH and greeting each person, asking them about life, family, work, how you can pray for them, and especially how you can serve them. As we build these relationships, it helps to strengthen the bonds of trust, and that trust is fundamental in allowing an artistic collaboration to occur.

I encourage you to adopt the band. Be a "Sound Dad" (or Mom)! Take care of these guys and girls as if they were your own. Some of them may be hard to handle, but if you remember your own debt to Christ, I hope you will find the strength to love them anyway, as Christ constantly does for you. When they see us pouring ourselves out and submitting to Christ, (sacrificing our own sanity even!) they will begin to see a bigger image of Jesus through you. I promise you, this will begin to change the culture and nature of your relationship with your worship team.

Technical vs. Musical

Many of you may have been musicians before you became sound techs, but there are quite a few of us that are more technically gifted than musical, which could be a real disadvantage. If you don't have a natural ear for music, an ear that is developed by being actively involved with it, it's pretty hard to develop the listening skills that are required for mixing. On the other hand, you may be all musical with very little technical gifting.

The relationships we develop with the worship team are especially important. As they grow, your perception of the band will change from problems to partners. If you find yourself lacking in an area, you will be more comfortable to ask them questions to help you grow in skill and knowledge.

If you find yourself in either of these places, don't be afraid to acknowledge this weakness and ask for help! You're partnered with the worship team. You are not alone! Ask questions; ask for helpful criticism from the band, the leadership, and the congregation. Study and learn as much as you can from more experienced musicians and sound engineers. The art of sound mixing is just that: Art. An artist has to practice and hone his craft. And for the technically or musically challenged, it might just be a matter of putting in the time to learn your craft.

Set aside some time with your worship leader to talk through what the mix should be like. Ask for examples of songs (preferably ones in the band's repertoire) that they feel are mixed well. Then critically listen to each recording. Try to listen for each individual instrument, to every aspect of the mix until you are able to identify every instrument and harmony. And as you do this, think about how it's layered in the mix. What frequency ranges are you hearing? What's the loudest and when? Developing a critical ear for mixing can take a long time, but it starts with simply listening.

Sound Advice

I kind of want to warn you about searching online for sound advice, technical wisdom, and education. You can find just about anything you want and everyone will have a different opinion about what sounds good. (I fully acknowledge this book is full of my opinions!) But be quick to discern what is helpful and what might be an empty opinion.

A lot of the information you can find online may not actually apply to your situation. The sources and materials that are telling you to "always" do something a certain way may be using very different sound boards, amps, outboard gear, mics, and speakers. Keep in mind these questions as you research: "Does this actually apply to my situation?" and "Will this help further the gospel or will it just make me look better?"

Chapter Six

Burnout

Looking for Affirmation

I had been working at Cornerstone Church in Simi Valley, California for about a year or so. I had come in, relabeled things, retuned the system, and worked with the band. Things were going well. The pastors were pleased with the sound and I didn't get a whole lot of complaints (at least, I didn't think so).

As the year went on, I began to doubt if things were actually going well, because I wasn't getting compliments like I had when I first started. Things were pretty automatic and I tried to rest in the confidence that the leadership had put in me, but it wore on me as time went on.

I consistently doubted my mixes and didn't feel happy with anything I was doing. I was pretty hard on myself and held a lot of negativity in my heart, simply because I didn't know if I was doing a good job anymore. There's an old saying about sound production, "If no one says anything, then everything is good." It's a nice thought in theory, and for the most part it is true. But as many sound engineers know, a compliment for us is a bit like a blind squirrel finding an acorn. It simply doesn't happen that often.

After several months of mixing without a word about anything, positive or negative, I began to feel pretty tired and a little bitter. Then one Sunday, Pastor Todd Nighswonger walked by the sound booth and asked me how I was doing. I told him I was tired, didn't know if I was doing a good job anymore, and honestly felt a little burned out. So the following Monday, Todd took to me to Panera Bread (which was apparently the alternative office for Cornerstone Church). I told Todd about how I wasn't receiving compliments, or even criticism anymore, and I was questioning how I was doing.

Todd told me that I needed to stop looking for my affirmation from the pastors, worship leaders, band, or the congregation. I needed to find that affirmation from my heavenly Father. And while I knew, as most of us do, that the only affirmation we really need is from the Lord, Todd's approach to it changed my life.

Finding Affirmation

Todd told me that I could find my affirmation through discipleship. Discipleship? I'm just a sound guy, and discipleship sounds like such a "pastoral" thing. But Todd helped me think of my sound position as pastoral; I'm there to help take care of the body and those I disciple. He told me that if I brought people into the sound booth to train, I could also talk through the gospel in our time together.

By being involved in their lives, I would find the affirmation I had been longing for. I would begin to feel the approval of my heavenly Father as I did what Jesus has commanded: make disciples.

To me, this was a mind-blowing concept! I had never thought of my job outside the context of worship and just...production. But it made perfect sense. I could train people in the technical art of mixing sound, while being intentional about the gospel. I could help others walk through their own struggles of faith and life.

I felt very ill-equipped at the time to even talk about the gospel, and some days I still do, but I just started doing it. The Holy Spirit was faithful to give me the right words at the right time. I just started sharing what God was doing in my life and tried to weave it into conversations with the people I was training. That M7cl sure heard a lot of conversations about sound, tech stuff, geekdom, and especially about the gospel.

When I saw that light bulb switch on as my trainees understood a technical concept or were encouraged by a new aspect of the gospel, I felt affirmed that I was pleasing God Himself and that affirmation finally satisfied my soul. A thousand hands of applause couldn't compare to watching my volunteer nod in understanding as we both caught a greater glimpse of Jesus. This was the affirmation my soul had longed for all along and I didn't even know it needed. Affirmation through discipleship may be the best way to give a burned-out engineer the energy and desire to come back to sound.

The Effects of Discipleship

When we wrap our heads around the idea that we can actually be intentional disciple-makers as well as sound engineers, it helps to lessen the effects of our own burnout. We no longer make the job all about "me," it becomes about pouring into another person. We no longer say, "Look what I can do!" but instead, "Look at this person! Look what they can do!"

It means we've become accountable to someone else, which can be humbling. It also greatly lessens the pressure of being the only sound person and loosens the grip of territorialism. Information is now shared instead of hoarded by an individual. It's scary at first, but the beauty of discipleship is that it's community, unity, and affirmation all in one.

Discipleship also fulfills another need of the church—sound volunteers—which as many of us know, finding these elusive creatures can be pretty difficult. I try to make it clear to my volunteers that I am intentionally training them so that they will eventually be able to train someone else.

For those of us that have been locked away in that booth for far too long, I know this concept is a breath of fresh air. This job can be about more than just running sound; it can be about discipleship and furthering the gospel in your own life. Disciple-ship forces us to no longer be idle observers in the gospel, but active participants.

Young people are a natural consideration for discipleship. As a teenager I would have loved to have had someone take an interest in me, to teach me sound and speak the gospel into my life. It's an amazing opportunity for us, as believers and as sound engineers, to have an impact on the next generation. There are so many practical teaching moments that happen during the course of set up, sound check, services, and strike; I'm talking about technical and gospel moments here. When you start making disciples, you'll find that these moments go hand and hand. As we talk about the technical side of sound, we also remind them that it's more important to give glory to God in all we do.

The Introvert in All of Us

There may be some of you that are completely intimidated by the idea of sharing your faith, and I understand that the sound position often attracts introverts (according to my wife, I'm one of them). Because of the nature of what we do, we don't have to physically interact with a whole lot of people. We basically hide out in the back of the room. But Jesus has called us to make disciples among the nations and wherever we are.

For the longest time I thought the gospel required us to be extroverted. But the reality is that God has uniquely created us, ex-troverted and introverted alike, to serve in His kingdom. The gos-pel doesn't demand that we walk up to every stranger we see and share the gospel. What the gospel does ask of us is to "walk in the Spirit" (Gal. 5:16). The pressure isn't on us, it's on the Holy Spirit and when the Spirit prompts us to go, speak, and interact, we do it. We don't have to sweat about whether we're missing opportunities to share the gospel. All we really have to do is "keep in step with the Spirit" (Gal. 5:25).

When the Holy Spirit asks you to, I encourage you to walk in faith and let someone in. It can be all about the technical stuff at first. Then as you get to know the other person, you can begin pointing them back to Jesus. You don't have to have a seminary degree to share the gospel nor am I asking you to unpack its full weight each Sunday. Just be in someone's life and share your own. I promise, if you will take these steps to become a disciple-maker and consistently ask the Holy Spirit to give you the right words when you need them, He will be faithful (Luke 12:12).

> And Jesus came and said to them, "All authority in heaven and on earth has been given to Me. Go therefore and make disciples of all nations, baptizing them in the name of the Father and of the Son and of the Holy Spirit, teaching them to observe all that I have commanded you. And behold, I am with you always, to the end of the age." (Matt. 28:18-20)

Chapter Seven

Sound Weighted in the Gospel

The Emotional Line

Knowing what actually sounds right can be hard to learn. It's a matter of practice, patience, making mistakes, learning from others, and time. But we need to know what we're aiming for. Having a strong relationship with your worship leader, collaborating with the worship team, and having others give you constructive criticism are very important, but the point is to remember whom we're serving. When we do our job correctly and worshipfully, it's as if we're providing the most accurate canvas for the worship team to paint the biggest picture of Jesus that they can, a canvas to proclaim the truth of the gospel through song.

> Great truth deserves great emotion.
> —Matt Papa

(When we encounter beautiful music, we feel an emotional response and when we encounter the gospel, it stirs up an even more powerful sensation; but when they come together we begin to sense the fount of all beauty: Jesus.)

As we mix, we walk an invisible emotional line. If the mix isn't loud enough or full enough it doesn't move us and we don't emotionally connect. If the mix is too loud or brash, it's a distraction and we don't emotionally connect. So we look for that line, for the beauty of what's happening in the room. And we let the mix be a part of that, driving it and supporting it, looking out into the body to see if people are engaging in worship and letting that be our guide. Sometimes I mix until I emotionally connect with the music and begin to worship with my voice. In that moment I'm overwhelmed by the beauty of the music and the beauty of the gospel. I try to stay there as long as I can to exalt the Holy God.

Mixing in the Spirit

There is an element to mixing that I've only begun exploring in the last couple of years as a sound engineer. I've been in situations where I know the mix isn't right and I'd realize I was mixing in a selfish way that wasn't serving the body. I would pray in my heart, surrender my mix to the Lord, and even take my hands off the board. I've seen Him take some bad mixes and do something I couldn't. In those moments, I could hear the Holy Spirit take control of all of the 20,000 frequencies I thought were under my control. I'd listen and think to myself, "I'm not doing that." It's a powerful and humbling feeling.

I also believe there's an element to asking the Holy Spirit what to do with the mix. Intentionally ask the Spirit, "What should I change?" or "What do you want?" It may come across as hokey, but consider the Holy Spirit as another relationship we have to partner with as we mix. Sometimes the best thing we can do is just lay the ground work for the Holy Spirit. Do your job well, so the Spirit can come in and work in every heart in the room. Pray through your mixes and be open to the leading of the Spirit.

Working Out Your Own Salvation

"Work out your salvation." That phrase always baffled me while growing up. It seemed legalistic and counterintuitive to the gospel. Why do I have to work for my salvation? Salvation is just grace through faith, right? In a sermon called "Living A Life That Matters, Living Reverently," Francis Chan delves into this phrase which Paul uses in Philippians. It isn't work FOR your salvation, but work OUT your salvation. This phrase, "work out," is more evocative of something like mining, in the way you "work out" the gems and jewels of the mountain.

> Therefore, my beloved, as you have always obeyed, so now, not only as in my presence but much more in my absence, work out your own salvation with fear and trembling, for it is God who works in you, both to will and to work for His good pleasure. (Phil. 2:12-13)

When we come to Christ, we have the opportunity to get as much out of our salvation as we want; to mine the riches of God, to know Him more, to find new ways to serve and love Him, to grow closer, to see His glory, and then to see ourselves refined and sanctified in the process. We do this daily because we're compelled by His goodness and grace. God shows us all that's available to us through Him.

And for those of us who serve through sound in our churches, we have another way to work out our salvation. Being a sound engineer is about so much more than just pushing faders. It's about finding out as much as you can about God and His attributes in what you do, learning what it looks like to follow Christ and how to be more like Him, seeing His glory and worshiping Him with all of your heart, and making disciples—all from behind a sound board.

Serving your church is now a way for you to live out the gospel, to communicate it and grow in it. Where before you might have been in over your head or a know-it-all, you can now become part of a new category, a sound engineer that is secure and confident. Praise no longer defines you and negative feedback is no longer taken personally because your identity is in Christ.

You can set your ego aside and actually hear the heart behind what people say, whether complaint, criticism, or compliment. You're making disciples and training them to do the job quickly, efficiently, humbly, and beautifully. And now that the gain structure of your heart is set, you can truly begin to worship.

Sound in the Gospel

I was at a Matt Papa event, sitting at FOH. The event had just ended and a young man came up to the booth and introduced himself. He asked me, "So do you get to worship while mixing?" I was baffled for a moment before I realized what he was asking. The disconnect between mixing and worship was never more accurately communicated.

He was basically asking if I got to sing while I mix. I told him that sometimes I do sing, but mostly I listen. Quickly I explained that everything I do as a sound engineer can be worship. Every knob I turn or fader I push, every interaction with the band or a volunteer can be worship. It's my deepest desire to communicate the gospel with my actions and my words, to let everything that flows out of my heart be an act of worship.

I pray that you now see that when you serve your church through sound, (or in any venue/position) that you are there to worship in EVERYTHING you do. Worship is not an isolated event that happens for 20 minutes each Sunday. We were made to worship.

My prayer for you (and for myself) is that you would see a bigger image of Jesus, that you would take up your cross and follow Him daily, and when you see your old flesh wanting to take control, that you'd go the extra mile to make sure you crucify it. I pray that your vision is widened and that you see more of His glory. And I pray that you will continue to look for this glory, behold it, and even listen for it.

Always consider where your heart is set. The next time you reach up to adjust the gain knob, think to yourself in the midst of the chaos:

"Is my heart Sound in the Gospel?"

"Unfortunately most people don't recognize good sound,
but even more unfortunately...
everyone can recognize bad sound."

-Paul Rice

Part II
The Toolbox

Gain Structure

If gain structure is so fundamental, how do we go about setting it? Unfortunately there are several misconceptions on how to use gain. A lot of people were taught to set faders to zero, then turn up the gain knob until they get "enough" signal. The problem with this is that it makes gain structure entirely relative to you!

If you're trying to run monitors, in-ears, Avioms, effects, or any number of sends from FOH, you may not have enough signal to go around. Monitors can be compromised when run from FOH if gain is not correctly set. There is a better way to set up your gain structure that will be more foundational, give you more headroom, and help you craft a bigger and fuller mix.

The Plumbing Analogy

As a kid, when my family went on vacation for a couple of weeks, my dad would give me this really big wrench and have me shut off the water to our house. I would go out to the valve on the side of the house and turn it as far to the left as I could to stop the flow of water. When we got back home from vacation, the first thing I did was turn the valve back on. If I turned it all the way back to the right, when my mom went to turn on the faucet, she'd get sprayed with water, but if I barely turned it on, the water would just drip. I usually had to check the pressure in the sink, go back outside and adjust it until it was right.

Signal flow is like water flowing through pipes. We're always trying to send our signal somewhere. The gain knob is like the shut off valve, controlling how much signal is allowed through. Keep the plumbing analogy in mind when you set input gain structure for each channel.

To begin setting the gain structure on an individual channel, leave the channel fader down, the gain knob at the top of the channel all the way to the left (off), and the master fader at zero.

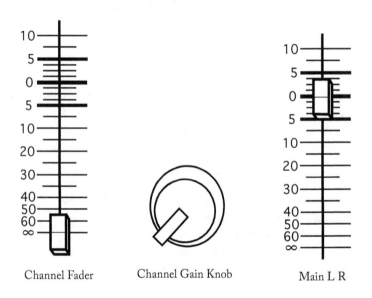

Channel Fader   Channel Gain Knob   Main L R

Ask the musician/vocalist to play/sing something at "performance level" (not just a "Check one, two") with the channel fader still down, so that no sound is coming out yet. Now press the PFL (Pre-Fader Listen), or Solo button on your board. Then slowly turn up the channel's gain until the PFL meter (usually located on the right side of an analog board) begins to register the input averaging around zero or "unity" (usually you'll see green and some yellow lights) on your PFL meter (due to dynamics, it will fluctuate a little above and below and that's perfectly okay).

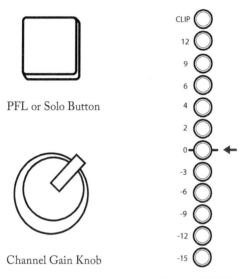

PFL or Solo Button

Channel Gain Knob

Analog PFL Meter

This sets the gain structure for that particular channel and the process repeats for each channel you use. Each board (analog and digital) has a different layout for how input levels are metered. Definitely consult your sound board's manual to locate your PFL or Solo meters if you have any trouble.

Digital Zero

For those of us who were trained on analog boards, keep in mind that there is a digital conversion factor. On sound boards like the Yamaha M7cl or Behringer X32 there isn't a zero on the input meter! A very easy and practical translation for setting gain structure on these boards is to set your input level to around -15 or about ¾ of the way up the meter where zero would be on an analog board.

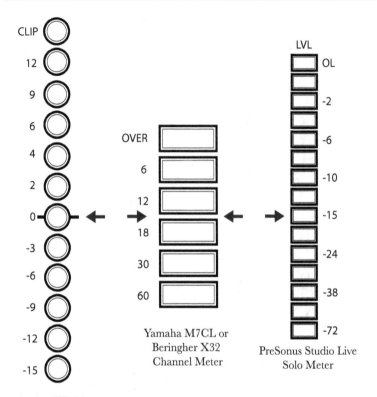

CLIP

12

9

6

4

2

0

-3

-6

-9

-12

-15

Analog PFL Meter

OVER

6

12

18

30

60

Yamaha M7CL or
Beringher X32
Channel Meter

LVL

OL

-2

-6

-10

-15

-24

-38

-72

PreSonus Studio Live
Solo Meter

If you try to set your channel to zero on a digital board, you'll
have clipping and distortion. Some would say you should turn the
gain up just until it clips and then back it down. And while there
isn't anything necessarily wrong with that, you'll have an easier time
fighting feedback and getting the faders naturally into higher fader
resolutions if you do follow the practical ¾ or -15 rule for situations where monitors are run from FOH, as it allows enough signal
to pass for both the FOH mix and monitor/Aviom style mixers.

Faders

When gain is properly set, you will consistently know how
much sound is going to come out when you push up the fader, and
you'll know you have plenty of headroom. It's completely okay if

the channel fader isn't sitting at zero. Think of the faders as paint-brushes: when you paint you move your brushes! It's okay if they're kind of all over the place.

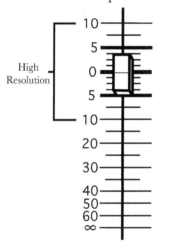

If you look at the numbers on a fader, you will see that they increase incrementally the higher you get. When the fader is around zero (about ¾ the way up) you get into what is called "high resolution."

If your fader is near the bottom, the volume increases anywhere from two to five decibels (dB) every time you touch it. When the fader is in high resolution, it only increases one dB at a time, which is really cool.

Some people think all of the faders need to be at zero so that the whole mix will be in this higher resolution, but that shouldn't necessarily be the end goal. Setting gain structure via the input level, will give you a lot more to work with, and the fader will most likely end up in higher resolution as you mix.

Give it Some Gas!

Another important aspect of gain structure is where to set the master, or main/left/right (output) fader (this is what Paul Rice called the "Gas!" fader). I've seen a lot churches try to throttle back the sound by turning down the master fader. I've even seen some people tape it into position about ¼ of the way up, which is evidence of a terrible misunderstanding of gain structure. The master fader should be kept at zero and the other channel faders mixed to the desired volume level.

So, I Just Lied to You...

To summarize, I've just told you to set your input gain levels around zero, mix with your channel faders, and have your master fader at zero. But here's the reality, there are situations where this isn't always the case (please don't throw the book out the window).

There really isn't anything wrong with pulling the master fader down a few decibels, as long as you're not killing the mix, and it can help control overall volume. There will also be times when you won't necessarily be able to get your input gain to zero (due to feedback issues). This usually happens with pastor's mics, lapel mics, choir mics and other condenser mics. These input levels might end up living just under zero. It depends on your sound system and how it's set up. If you're primarily using dynamic mics, getting your input gain to zero will almost never be a problem.

Gain structure also has to be set every step of the way, from the sound board, to the digital signal processor, crossovers, and finally the amps. It's the best possible scenario when all of these components are set to zero/unity (otherwise known as nominal). But there will be times where there have to be compromises due to the size of the sound system, room, and coverage.

As you gain more experience as an engineer, you will begin to identify when and where you need to adjust your settings. Just remember, don't make gain structure relative to you. Give yourself enough input signal to work with. Listen to your mix and look at your channels. Let the input level be your standard. If you follow these basic steps of gain structure, I promise your mix will already start in the ballpark.

Chapter Nine

Equalization

Potter Analogy

So let's move on from gain structure and talk about equalization, or EQ. When you're mixing in the studio, you might boost some frequencies, compress something really hard, and shape the EQ this way or that until you get what you want.

It's a bit like being a potter: you start with a piece of clay, then you shape and mold it. You can add more clay to it if you want and you keep working it until you have your super cool pot of awesomeness. (This was in no way a drug reference.) The problem is that when you try to EQ the same way in a live setting, you can get yourself into a lot of trouble.

Say you had a vocalist singing his or her heart out. You think to your self, "Self, I think that vocal needs to be sharper and crisper." So you reach for the EQ knob and boost the 2k and 16k frequencies into the vocal.

But what you forgot to consider is that the drums are right behind the vocalist and you've just boosted all the cymbals in the vocal mic, which is now painfully feeding back into the sound system.

Marble Sculpture Analogy

Things from the studio world don't always translate into the live realm. Live sound is more akin to sculpting than pottery. Setting gain structure is like choosing the width and height of a block of marble. If the gain structure is too low, your block will be really small. When you chisel into it you may not have enough to work with or it may break in half because it's too narrow or thin.

A properly set gain structure gives you a nice big piece of marble to sculpt. When you EQ in a live setting, you will almost always reduce or take away from the EQ strip. If you want that vocalist to be sharper and crisper you might want to look at cutting some of the lows and low-mids. And since you have a big piece of marble, you can chisel deep into it without breaking the sculpture.

Sweep and Destroy

Once you start learning frequencies, you'll hear them everywhere! And over time you'll be able to identify certain frequencies and ranges. Whenever you think you hear something you want to change with the EQ, take a guess at what range it's in. Use the Q knob on your EQ (used to widen or narrow the frequency range) and set it to the point that you're only controlling a few frequencies in that range, which is called narrow Q. (Note: Most analog boards don't have a Q knob but have a permanently set medium Q.)

Then go to the EQ gain section, boost it a couple dB and use the frequency knob to sweep back and forth until you confirm what you heard. Listen for the most offending frequencies, go back to the EQ gain knob, and cut the frequency a few dB. Then widen out the Q until it sounds right to ensure a more natural sound. Narrow Q's can cause some small phasing issues if the cut is too deep, and the sympathetic frequencies on either side might pop out and cause trouble.

Do this in the necessary ranges (low, low-mid, high-mid, high) until you pull out the offending frequencies and are left with a natural, accurate sound. Remember to think critically about what to adjust. You may not have to do anything on some of the ranges, most often you just need small tweaks on two or three of them.

Sweep and Destroy Examples

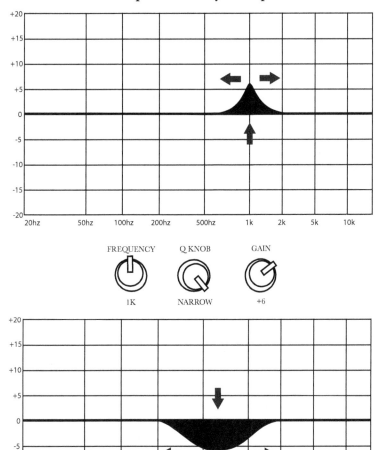

Only use this technique during sound check. Sweeping and destroying during a service would be pretty distracting! If you need to make an EQ change in the middle of service, find the range you think the problem is in, cut it just a bit, and sweep it back and forth until it sounds better.

As you learn how to sweep and destroy, and especially as you begin to recognize frequency ranges, always run your EQ changes through a mental filter. Ask yourself, "Am I pulling too much out? Does it sound natural? Does it sound like the source?" Learn to trust your ears, not just the settings on the board. If it sounds bad to you, then it probably sounds bad! But if it sounds good, leave it alone! Don't overwork yourself on EQ.

High Pass Filter

The "High Pass Filter" (or HPF) is an important tool that increases the bandwidth and headroom in your sound system. You choose a frequency in the low range so that every frequency beneath it is rolled off and everything above it is allowed to pass (hence the "high pass"). The HPF basically tells the speakers, "Hey, you don't have to worry about these low frequencies on this channel; we don't need them."

When we try to push too much through the system, it creates distortion because the speaker just can't keep up. The HPF allows us to put just a little bit more through the system. Just about every channel we use will have the HPF engaged at some level, as it can be adjusted.

When a speaker has to produce low frequencies like 100hz and lower, you can physically start to see the speaker cone moving. When it gets as low as 60hz to 20hz you can see it move a lot! (This is what destroys speakers, by the way.) When the high frequencies go through the speaker, they move so fast that they are actually invisible to the naked eye.

There is a similar tool called the "Low Pass Filter" (or LPF) which does the exact opposite of the HPF; it rolls the highs out of a channel. It can be helpful to use the LPF to pull out the very high frequencies that might be giving you feedback trouble. But you

The High Pass Filter

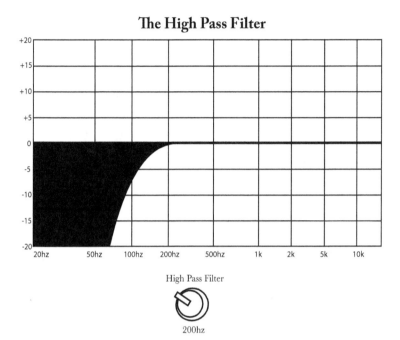

High Pass Filter

200hz

should only use it as a temporary fix until you can identify and cut the troublesome feedback frequencies. If you use too much of the LPF, you will begin to lose intelligbility on that channel from cutting high-end frequencies.

Sound System Tuning

An important aspect of equalization is system EQ, which is used to pull the trouble frequencies out of the entire system. System tuning is usually done by professionals and if you want to play around with this, please keep in mind that you can seriously hurt your system as well as your ears!

Professional system tuning is often done with RTA (Real Time Analyzing Software), which is basically a microphone you put in the room that is then run into a computer which visually shows you how all of the frequencies are interacting in the room.

It's a very useful tool, but can also be terribly complicated and far too easy to mess up, especially in the wrong hands. You can have everything EQ'd the way the program tells you is "correct" and it can still sound bad. You have to trust your ear, not what a computer screen tells you is right.

On the other hand, RTA software is very important for big touring productions to be able to see how their system is interacting with a room. I think I can safely assume that most of you reading this don't have a million dollar line array sound system, so let me suggest another way.

Vocal System Tuning

A far simpler and, in my opinion, more effective and practical way of system tuning is through the human voice. The advantage of this is that once you get the voice to sound natural, all the other instruments seem to fall into place (which is interesting to think about in light of God's design of the human voice!)

First you must locate your system EQ, which is usually either a piece of outboard gear next to your sound board or locked away in the digital signal processor typically found near the amp box. (Note: The best tools for system tuning are a parametric EQ paired with a graphic EQ, either in your digital processor or on your digital sound board. Use the parametric EQ for your primary system tuning and then the graphic EQ for anything that's left.)

Once you've located and gotten into your system's EQ, flatten it out (no frequencies boosted or cut), then plug your main vocal mic into a channel on the board. Make sure the EQ on that channel is off or flat, with no HPF and your subs off. Set your gain structure on that channel (remember the ¾ or -15 rule) and bring the fader up to as close to zero as you can and just talk to yourself. It's okay. Everybody does it.

Walk around the room and talk, or sing if you'd like. It's important for a sound engineer to get comfortable talking into a sound system. It can be awkward at first, but it's good to learn how your voice interacts in different systems and rooms, as it gives you a standard to listen for.

With the parametric or graphic EQ (or whatever EQ you have), begin pulling the bad frequencies you hear in your voice. Boost a frequency to confirm what you hear and then cut it using the sweep and destroy technique. Pull out any muddiness, honkiness, harshness, and extra sibilance in your voice. The frequencies you are changing should be on the main output, not the individual channel. Typically, the parametric EQ will be used first, and then if you have a graphic EQ, you can use that for more detailed fine-tuning.

Continue until your voice sounds entirely natural with no help from the channel EQ strip, (even with the HPF disengaged!) then have someone else talk into the microphone and compare the results. You want it to sound big and full, not muddy or sharp, just pleasant.

Please remember that every room is different as well as each sound system, so the example on the following page is NOT meant to be copy/pasted in your system. I offer this example because I've seen far too many system EQs with a "happy face" (lows boosted, mids cut, highs boosted). And despite the name, it doesn't make for a happy sound system.

Possible System Tuning on a Graphic EQ

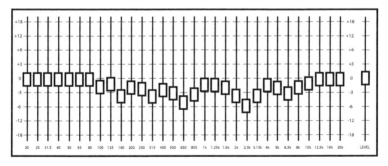

Note the multiple notches and wide Q's via thumbing (pulling three frequencies at once). Thumbing is important on a graphic EQ, because if you only pull one frequency it may cause phasing issues and may not sound natural. (Thumbing does not apply to analog boards that have set Q's.)

Depending on the quality of your speakers, it might be helpful to pull or shelve some of the low frequencies, as your subwoofers will handle that range. Most high quality speakers, or top boxes, will probably already have some form of a crossover in the box that keeps them from getting into the lower ranges. Experiment with pulling these frequencies and see how they interact with your subwoofers.

Subwoofers

Once you've got your speakers tuned, move on to the subwoofers. As I've said, subs handle the low end, usually 100hz and below, which allows the top boxes to be used exclusively for the low-mid to high frequencies. If your system is set up correctly the subs should have a crossover either in a digital signal processor or a physical crossover unit in the amp rack. If the subs are "active," the amp will be in the sub box itself. Look at the back of the sub for the available options. Most active subs automatically crossover at the correct frequency.

Some sound systems use the subwoofers in line with the signal flow from the main speakers, which means that the signal goes through the main speakers and then into the subs. While there certainly isn't anything wrong with this setup, I personally prefer to have the subs configured to run off of an aux send (post fader). This means you choose to send particular channels to the subs as well as the main speakers. This is helpful for the kick, toms, bass guitars and keyboards. It helps to clean up the sound and offers feedback control.

If your subs are in line with the main speakers, turn off the top boxes (the mid and high range speakers) until you can hear just the subs. If your system is configured to run the subs off an aux send, set that aux to pre-fader and pull down the faders so you can isolate the subs. If you listen to music and you can hear vocals in the subs, they are crossed over too high. You should only hear the very low rumble of vocals; it shouldn't be intelligible.

You'll need to look at the crossover settings and check to see that they are set for 100hz, at minimum, and below. (Some subs are set for lower, around 80hz.) As you listen to the subs, you might notice some resonant frequencies in the room. Using another graphic EQ, begin to identify the trouble frequencies. Be very careful about over-boosting, as you can quickly damage your subs. Most will operate just fine with just the crossover and no graphic EQ, but again, every room reacts differently.

If you don't happen to have a crossover for your subs, it's possible to use a graphic EQ to fake a crossover (shown below), although it won't do as well as a digital signal processor with a crossover. If you have lower quaility or smaller than 18" subs, it might be helpful to pull out some of the sub-octave frequencies (20hz-40hz) that are going to the subs to help protect them from damage. High-end subwoofers should be able to handle every-thing down to 20hz.

Possible Subwoofer Tuning on a Graphic EQ

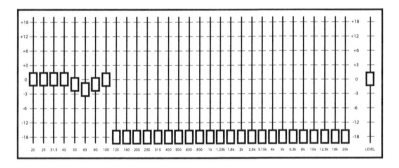

After everything is dialed in, turn all the speakers back on, play some of your favorite music and see how it sounds. Listen to how the top boxes and subwoofers are working together. Try to limit yourself to pulling maybe only two to three more frequencies. Keep in mind that most music is a mastered product. You could try to dig out every suspected evil frequency, but you might end up making the system too brittle and thin (think of the marble sculpture analogy).

Usually the less expensive your sound system is, the more fre-quencies you will have to pull for it to sound correct in your room. You have to stop yourself every once in a while and ask, "Am I pulling too much?" Though some sound systems will surprise you with how good they sound without much work.

This way of system tuning is meant to get your system in the ballpark. It won't be perfect, but it will be workable and user-friendly for volunteers. If you've tuned the system correctly (and I have complete faith in you), you won't have to pull as much on the individual channel EQs. And if a specific instrument needs a small EQ boost you can now safely do that.

Monitors

The best way to make a band happy is to make sure they can hear themselves! Monitors can be speakers (called wedges) on the floor pointed back toward the musicians, wireless in-ear monitors, Ethernet-based sub-mixers called Avioms, or a combination of all of the above. Sometimes there are entire sound boards dedicated to monitor mixing.

Monitor wedges can be a huge nuisance for sound engineers because of the way they can color the mix with their stage volume. For most churches, wedges are run from FOH. Of course the worship team needs to hear themselves to do what they need to do, but you need to help them understand that the volume needs to be at a conservative enough level that it doesn't overpower the FOH mix.

These can be very tricky conversations, because the monitor is often a confidence booster and you can't just take that away. Walk carefully in these conversations and show as much grace as you can. If a vocalist or musician wants more of themselves in their monitor, it might be beneficial to turn other things down instead of turning that person up. Also consider where the monitor is placed (if it's not an in-ear system). A simple tweak can make all the difference.

Monitor wedges need to be tuned using the same technique I described in system tuning. They also require their own graphic or parametric EQ inserted on each mix. The difficult thing with tuning wedges is that it can be a two-person job, with one person talking and listening to the monitor while another person makes the EQ changes. But with digital boards and the wonders of tablets and apps, you can pull frequencies and talk at the same time! So when tuning wedges, talk into your main vocal mic while standing in front of it, pulling frequencies on the EQ while increasing the send to the monitor.

This time try to get as much gain out of the mic before it causes feedback. You will typically have to pull frequencies more aggressively to reduce the chance of feedback during the performance. And remember to turn things up slowly. You're generating feedback on purpose! You do this to give yourself as much headroom in the monitor send as you can get.

While you go through this process, the monitor volume will be louder than what the musician will actually need. That way when a musician or vocalist asks for more, you can give it to them, hopefully without feedback. You also have to make sure you don't pull too many frequencies, which will cause it to sound muffled or thin. Once you're done pulling frequencies, back the send down to the monitor to what you feel is a good starting volume for your band.

Wireless IEM

Wireless in-ear monitor systems are great for musicians and FOH sound engineers, especially if you also have ear buds, so you can accurately hear what they're hearing. You almost always send signal to any type of monitors PRE-fader, so that when you make changes to the FOH mix, you don't also change their monitor mix. Some digital boards have the option to change the aux sends to the monitors to pre-EQ as well. They get a direct send before the equalizer in the signal flow, so they won't hear the changes made to the EQ.

This is particularly great for drummers and guitarists because it allows them to hear the tone from their instruments accurately. And if a vocalist or any musician wants a different overall tone in their ears (due to different quality ear buds), we can offer that through the parametric EQ on the aux send master for the monitors. This option is on most digital boards.

Compression is sometimes inserted on in-ear monitor mixes, but it comes down to a personal preference for the musician or vocalist. Compression can kill monitors if used incorrectly. It can cause trouble for vocalists in particular, who will over-sing in an attempt to hear themselves.

If you find yourself stuck on an analog board, you may not have pre-fader options on all the auxes and you probably don't have a parametric EQ for your aux outs. In this case, you have to be very careful how you EQ, making as few changes as you can on the channel EQ strip. (You'll likely need to do more work on system tuning to find this balance.) lso, compression will be in the signal flow going to the monitors, so you'll have to use very light compression to get what you need in your FOH mix while not killing the monitor mix for the band. Compressing the main mix might be a better option than compressing specific channels.

Also note that sweeping and destroying can really damage eardrums if your musicians have in-ear monitors, especially if you don't let them know you're about to change something. Make sure you communicate everything you're doing to the band through your talkback mic. It's easy for the band to get lost and confused about what they're hearing in sound check. Remember to take care of them!

Chapter Ten

Mixing

Mixing 101

To create the biggest and fullest mix possible, you need to think fundamentally. Look to the "Rock & Roll Basics."

1.) Kick
2.) Bass
3.) Snare
4.) Guitars
5.) Keys
6.) Vocals

This lists the instruments in order of foundational priority (not the order of volume level) as you begin to mix, which will set you up for a big, full sound.

Start with the kick. Get it to the level that you want, then bring in the bass guitar. The kick and bass should live around the same volume because they fundamentally work together as the foundation of the mix. Next bring in the snare. If you listen to a lot of music you've probably noticed that the snare is typically a predominate instrument. Set the snare volume on top of the kick and bass. Bring in the electric and acoustic guitars and you'll hear the mix begin to fill out. Then add the keys, the glue of the mix.

Finally, bring in the vocals and set them on top of everything. The distance between the vocals and the band should sound natural and creative, but in a worship setting, the vocals need to be heard clearly above the rest of the mix. If there are additional instruments, they can be added into this priority list based on what frequency range they cover. For example, add a violin or banjo to the list with the guitars.

Imagine your mix is a clear bucket. As you look at it from the side, the kick is at the bottom, then the bass, snare, guitar, keys, and the vocals near the top of the bucket. You can clearly see each section. If you look at the bucket from the top, you can see through to each instrument. You always want to be able to hear everything you see on stage.

Circular Mixing

If you've ever been to a large concert and had to sit through an opening band, you might have noticed that they usually sound really bad compared to the headliner. The opening band often does not have much time to sound check and their sound engineer is pretty much creating the mix as they go. You could be listening and think, "Wow, I can't hear the snare or the electric guitar."

Then you start to hear the instruments come into the mix in the "Rock & Roll" list order. The mix keeps getting better and better and may actually sound decent by the last song. Of course by then the set is over, which is unfortunate for the opener, but that's the nature of concerts.

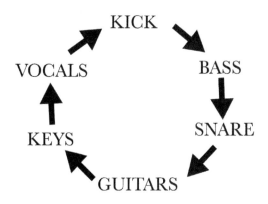

Using this priority list you will continually cycle through all the instruments on stage. The mix will naturally get better with every pass. A mix doesn't just happen, it takes time and effort. You don't just set it and forget it.

On one pass, think "Do I hear the floor tom? Nope." Then push up the floor tom and cycle through again. "Do I hear the keys? The synth?" Push it up. "Do I hear that background vocalist?" Push him or her up. "Is that electric guitar too loud? Probably." Turn it down.

Frankly we should always be working, always making sure all the instruments are in the proper place. Most importantly, think musically! Listen for what will best serve the song, what instrument drives it. Mixing is organic in nature; it ebbs and flows. If you're thinking to yourself, "But I don't know where the proper place is!" It's okay, don't forget that you are partnered with your worship leader. Ask questions, ask for help, get feedback from the band and your audience. Be willing to take the criticism. It will take time. Remember you don't have to do this alone.

Mixing Volume

Sound is, of course, very relative. What's loud to one person isn't loud enough for the next. When it comes to mix volume, it needs to be a decision that comes from the leadership. For us sound engineers, we must honor that decision and try to keep the mix within those guidelines.

For modern contemporary worship, my guideline at FOH is 85-90 dBA. Anything above that makes people feel like they're at a concert and a lower volume may cause a disconnect. The volume will naturally rise and fall, but I personally feel that an average of 90 dBA with a good, full sound is emotionally engaging and conveys beauty, although it's possible to have a full mix at lower volumes.

There's a psychological connection between volume level and full sound. If you're mixing and think it feels great, then suddenly mute your subs, you might find that your big, full mix now sounds brash and thin. Without the subs giving you low-end frequency coverage, your previous volume seems too loud. Bringing the subwoofers back in will reverse the effect and your ears will once again find the volume pleasing.

This also speaks into having enough low-end instruments in the mix, as well as what the subwoofer coverage looks like. Having enough subwoofers built into your sound system is fundamental in building a full mix; it isn't just about being louder.

Mixing well certainly involves an element of understanding the capabilities of your sound system and your band. If you attend a small church with two speakers on sticks, you can't try to sound like the big church next door with their giant line array sound system. I encourage you not to force a mix on your system and your congregation. You'll end up hurting one or the other. Embrace what God has blessed you with; take care of it and make the most of what you have. Create something beautiful.

Chapter Eleven

Dynamics and Effects

I have to be honest, I think it took a good five years before I really wrapped my head around what a compressor actually does. It's a difficult concept to understand and sound engineers have vastly different opinions on how and when it should be used, which can make it even more difficult to practically learn to use. By definition, a compressor reduces dynamic range. If the faders are our paint brushes, then compression is what makes our "broad" fader brushes more "fine."

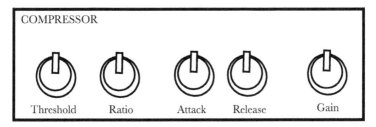

Most compressors have these 5 main control knobs:
threshold, ratio, attack, release, and gain.

Threshold and Ratio

The threshold and ratio knobs control how much dynamic range a channel has, which basically gives you more control over where each channel goes in the mix. Threshold corresponds to same numbers that mark the faders. If the threshold is set at -40, when a signal goes above that threshold on the fader, the compressor begins to affect the channel.

If the ratio is set to 2:1, it will also come into play. Then for every 2 dB that goes over the -40 threshold, it gets reduced by 1 dB. As the ratios increase (4:1, 6:1, 8:1) so does the reduction of signal, until ratio reaches ∞:1 and becomes a limiter. So if you set the ratio to 6:1, it would take 6 dB over the threshold for 1 dB to come out.

With these settings, that channel isn't going to get loud at ALL because its dynamic range is being squashed. (Note: I offer this threshold and ratio setup as pretty extreme example. If you experiment using this example as a base, you will certainly hear the compression.)

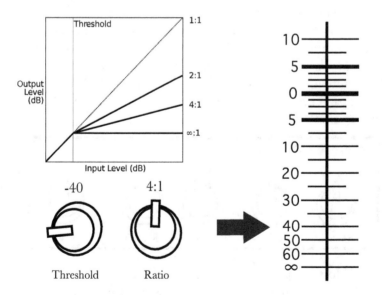

Attack and Release

The next components of compression are attack and release. Attack tells the compressor how quickly to start compressing once signal has reached the threshold. Release tells the compression how long to wait before resetting the ratio protocol after the threshold has been reached. Attack and release can also play into the tone and sustain of what you're compressing. A fast attack/slow release causes a darker sound and late attack/fast release causes a brighter sound. This is a result of how you control the attack frequencies (high and high-mid) and how much of them you allow to come out.

Make-Up Gain

When you reduce dynamic range, things get quieter. To make up for the volume reduction, increase the gain on the compressor. This is where the faders become "fine" paint brushes as you place that channel more precisely in the mix. (Note: Adding gain on the compressor will affect the gain structure on that channel and can sometimes add unwanted signal noise. Be sure to monitor the levels as you compress.)

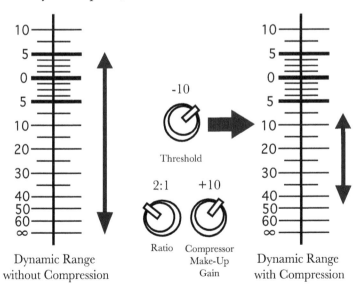

Dynamic Range without Compression

Ratio   Compressor Make-Up Gain

Dynamic Range with Compression

You tracking with me?

Sweet. Glad you're confused, I am too.

There are many schools of thought on compression, from "compress every single channel you have," to "only compress the main mix," to "don't use compression at all!"

Honestly, I don't think you can read a book to learn how to use a compressor, you need to just hear it for yourself and make up your own mind. Set aside some time, talk into a mic with compression inserted and play with the compressor controls until you wrap your head around it.

Remember, compression can be a great and powerful tool, and there are times when it is incredibly helpful. But dynamic range is a good thing! You don't want to take it all away. Dynamic range is what makes a mix sound big and full. Always ask yourself, "Am I compressing too much? Does it sound natural?" And consider if it will affect the monitor mix.

Gates

Gates work very similarly to compressors but entirely differently. (Don't you love it?) Gates function very much like a literal gate; there has to be some force in order to open it.

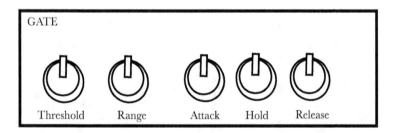

The threshold setting is the point at which the gate will open. Range sets how far the gate will close. The attack, hold, and release knobs control how fast it opens, how long it stays open, and how quickly it closes again, until the next instance where the signal goes above the threshold. Attack, hold, and release also give us control over the tone and sustain, much like a compressor.

Gates basically help clean up your sound by letting out only the signal you've chosen. This doesn't mean you should put them on everything, but there are some instruments they definitely help, namely kick drums, toms, and some noisy electric guitar amps. Again, set aside time to test different gate settings until it makes sense.

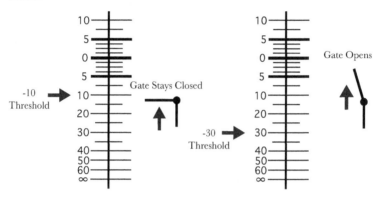

Reverb

Reverb is created by a device inserted into a sound board that creates artificial acoustics. It allows you to make a voice or instrument sound like it's in a bathroom or a giant arena. Reverb is one of my guilty pleasures and as a long-time Pink Floyd fan, I come by reverb naturally! I have to ask myself, or even someone else, "Is this too much verb or effect?" (The answer to which my wife always says, "YES!")

You should feel the emotion of reverb before you hear the actual effect. Bring up the reverb to where you begin to feel an emotional change in the mix. This emphatically goes for everything from vocals to snare drums. If you keep on pushing the reverb, it will begin to stick out, which means it's gone too far. That emotional line should be the guideline for how much reverb should be put into a mix.

The most common channels to get reverb are vocals, snares, toms, pianos, and acoustic instruments. Electric guitars and keyboards often have their own reverb effect, so ask your musicians if they are controlling their own reverb or not.

115

Delay

Where reverb is an affected signal, delay is the sampling of a signal. The same emotional guideline applies to delay, and less is often more, as too much delay can stick out like a fart in a library. There is nothing worse than a mistimed delay throw that goes on for several seconds. In most live productions, delay is primarily used just on vocals, but it's used often in studios for a number of situations. You should definitely communicate with your worship leader about how much reverb and delay to use on the vocals.

Coordinate those big moments where a good delay throw might be effective. By using the tap function of the delay unit, tap out the primary rhythm of the song (usually timed with the snare). This sets the delay repeat time and allows the delay to be in time with the song. Long delays are for the biggest moments, while short delays or "slap back" delays are meant for specific sounds and are often married with selected reverb settings.

Each reverb and delay unit is different. Some have tons of settings you can play with (too many to cover in this book!) and some are pretty basic. So again I encourage you to set some time aside to talk into a mic and experiment with the reverb and delay settings.

Chapter Twelve

Taking Care of the Band

The Drummer

While fostering and strengthening individual relationships with each of the band members is vital, you may find it harder to overcome differences with some more than others. In particular, the relationship with the drummer tends to be a common struggle for sound engineers.

Frankly, sometimes the drummer can be the bane of our very existence. The crashing cymbals, the random kick patterns, the heavy-handed hitting of every piece of the kit...it can destroy a mix. And if there's a drum shield, some drummers assume they get to play even louder! Young drummers think they can play as hard as they like because that's what they've seen in YouTube videos, and well...it is a lot of fun to beat the heck out of a drum kit every once and while!

The problem is that if a drummer doesn't play with enough "touch," they can out run the sound system (which means that the musician is louder than the system can handle). In a perfect world we'd all have big enough sound systems to overcome any stage volume, but most of us have just barely enough in our churches and venues.

The more experienced and professional drummers play with touch for tone and dynamics, not just for decibels (though there are times for that). They are also able to play dynamically to the size of the room, which can be a difficult and lengthy process for a drummer to learn. Patience with the drummer is key. It's important to build a relationship with your drummer that goes beyond the "drums."

We need to come around drummers and work with them as they develop their skill sets. We want them to see us not as a "Sound Nazi," but as a fellow artist who is completely invested in helping them create the best sound, tonally and dynamically, with their kits (which is also easier when the drummer has taken care of the kit and kept all of the drumheads in tune).

If there are tonal issues with a drum, it's always best to fix it at the source, either through tweaking the mic placement or through tuning (moon gels and gaff tape are particularly helpful). Don't beat yourself up with the EQ on the strip, fix it at the source and then come back to the EQ. You'll save yourself a major headache, and speaking of headaches…

I've often had young drummers whose thrashing about was unknowingly destroying my mix. It's easy to get frustrated and want to beat them with their own sticks (I'm just being honest here!) but the best thing to do is develop your relationship with him. Talk to him about his kit and how *he* wants to sound, because we're also trying to represent the tones and particular sounds of the drum kit in the most accurate way possible. If a drummer is too loud, I often ask him to pull back on the hardware (the cymbals) because that's usually the biggest culprit. Once you've developed this relationship and the drummer feels like you're on his team, he will be more open to these kinds of requests.

Most of the complaints received at FOH are about how loud and distracting the drums are (or stage volume in general). It's important to keep the elderly members in mind. You can cause actual physical discomfort with the low-end frequencies from the kick and bass. It can be wise to develop a kick sound that you "hear" more than "feel" by reducing sub frequencies and boosting attack frequencies, as well as to keep the bass guitar volume at a conservative level. But be careful not to sacrifice so much that it begins to hurt the mix by causing it to sound too thin.

You must be mindful of the congregation (especially the elderly) and of the expectations for the style of worship that the leadership is trying to guide you through. Having these conversations with your worship leader, drummer, and church leadership is paramount.

The Bass

The bass guitar is a fundamental element for any mix. Its tone is subtle and covers far more than just the low bass frequencies; there are high-mid and mid range frequencies used to develop its tone. Again, it's always best to fix bass tone at the source. You can ask your bass player for more attack or mid range to help it fit in the mix, or have them reduce some of their low-mids for clarity. There is a learning curve to the bass, so don't get discouraged if you don't hear the subtleties at first.

Bass players usually need the bass amp to live on stage with them, due to the difficulty of hearing the bass frequencies in their monitors. It is incredibly helpful for the bass player to be close enough to his amp to feel the bass as he plays. A lot of churches don't have bass amps and run the bass through a DI box, which really kills a lot of the warm tones for the bass. If a bass guitarist needs to run into a DI box, encourage him to invest in some bass pedals to help deepen the tone, because the voltage level sent through most DI boxes has the gain up so far that it creates extra noise in the signal. This can also happen with electric guitars.

The Electric Guitar

Learn what your guitar players are working with and what tone they'd like to have. You don't want to color their tone with your EQ! But if you find that your electric guitarist's tone is too bright or too dark, try to fix it at the source first. (Are you seeing a pattern here?) This doesn't mean you don't use the EQ on the channel, but there are a lot of things the guitarist can do for his or her tone if you just ask them.

Mic placement is also a great place to develop the tone. When the mic is placed toward the middle of the guitar amp's speaker cone, the tone will brighten and if you move it to the outer rim of the speaker cone it will darken. If you have two channels available to use for an electric guitar, you can dedicate two mics to a single guitar amp: one mic placed in the dark area and another in the bright area of the speaker cone. By moving one fader higher than the other, you have the ability to create bright or dark tones for the guitar without using the EQ strip.

Guitarists will usually appreciate your input about their tone because they don't know what it sounds like off stage. The more you work with them, the more you will deepen collaboration and trust.

It is true that electric guitarists need to turn up their amps to develop their tone. While this can create stage volume issues, there are a couple of solutions. They can run a long ¼ inch cable to their amps in a different room to create isolation and you can run mics out to the cabinets. If they leave their amps on stage, have them turn their amps around and use some sound dampening material to "dog house" the amp, basically building a box around the front of the amp.

The Acoustic Guitar

Then there is the simple acoustic guitar player, standing in the midst of a sea of electric guitars. Like Boss Ross standing on stage with AC/DC, it's easy for them get lost in the mix.

It's important to understand which instrument is driving a song. But it's also important to hear everything on stage. If the song is driven by electric guitars and the acoustic guitar is meant to be in the background, try to mix them until you can at least hear the strings being hit. Acoustic guitars can add as much rhythmically as muscially.

The acoustic guitarist usually has a pickup inside his guitar that plugs into a DI box. If you have issues with the tone, (I bet you know where I'm going with this) fix it at the source. If it's too bright or too mid-heavy, ask what he can do about it, until you arrive at a natural pleasing sound. Most acoustic guitars have a master volume knob. It's usually best to have it set at 75-100%, which gives you enough signal.

The Keyz

Much like everything else, if you have an issue with tone, fix it at the source and make sure they're sending you enough signal. (Are you tired of me saying that yet?) The keyboard player should also "set and forget" between 75-100% of his master volume. The sound engineer should be mindful of dynamic moments for the keys and control that for them.

There may be situations where the keyboard player would prefer to control the master volume personally, for example while "vamping" or "padding" under the pastor at the end of the sermon. There's nothing wrong with this as long as there's been communication between the keyboardist and the sound engineer about where the volume should be reset.

The keys can be the glue of your mix so don't neglect what they add. And remember to love your local keyboardist; it can get lonely out there in the back.

The Vocalists

Every voice is different and every singer has a different tonal quality, but one of the most common frustrations sound engineers have to deal with is the soft-spoken singer. You should encourage your vocalists to "eat the mic." Their lips should be about one or two inches away from the mic as they sing and then they can pull back for specific dynamic moments. When they do this, it gives you enough signal to work with and also gives them a more direct sound in their monitors. It's also important that they give performance level at sound check, not just "Check, check" or "One, two."

Some voices are boomy and some have an amazing amount of sibilance. Different types of mics lend themselves better to different types of vocals and it can be challenging to find the right mic for the right vocalist. You need to find the balance between what's best for the mix and what the vocalist is comfortable with. You also need to consider how much compression you put on the vocalist's channels. Most FOH boards that double as the monitor board don't have an option to bypass compression to the monitors, and over-compression will really hurt the vocalists in their monitors, causing them to over-sing to be able to hear.

Light compression with low ratios is almost always best on vocals and allows for dynamic moments. For the strong vocalists who might be hard to wrangle into a mix, collaborate with them on when to pull back from the mic and help them understand what might be hurting the mix. When you do this, you show them that you are invested in what they're doing and this will further deepen collaboration.

Sound Check

While the worship leader is in charge of the actual band rehearsal, it should be noted that the sound engineer should always be in charge of the sound check. The sound tech needs to step up and communicate what needs to happen. Make sure you have a good way to talk to your band, via a talkback mic which is routed into the floor monitors or wireless in-ear monitors. Always be careful to check the volume level of your talkback to the band. You don't want to hurt their ears while you're trying to run sound check.

The most helpful way to run a sound check is to go through each channel every time you have a rehearsal, politely asking the musician to play their instrument at performance level. During this time, check gain structure, slowly bringing up the channel in the mix while listening for any EQ issues. Once you feel good about that channel, ask the band who needs more or less of that instrument in their monitor.

It helps to go stage right to left, so you can quickly identify monitor mixes and the band can have an idea of where you're at with their monitor request. I often have band members keep their hands up until they are satisfied with their mix.

"Please" and "Thank you" goes a long way in this process. In fact, I encourage you to over-communicate with your band about what you're doing and what you're moving on to next. Be consistent in how you run sound checks. It will make for a quicker and easier process for everyone involved.

Stage Volume

For any instrument that needs to have an amplifier on stage, there is an easy rule to follow. Have the musicians turn up their amps until they are barely rattling the bottom of the snare drum. This creates a standard stage volume that they can easily find for themselves. Keep in mind this may not work in every room, especially in very small rooms. You and the band will have to make compromises. But if you have adequate sound coverage in your room, this rule should be easily followed.

The Pastors

Probably one of the most important aspects of the job is taking care of the pastors. Pastors' mics can cause quite a few problems for the sound engineer. The source of this problem is most often mic placement.

If the pastor is using a handheld mic and has the mic too far away from his mouth, then it will be problematic to get enough signal. (We all know pastors who are notorious for this.) They need to learn to lock their elbow in place to help keep the mic at a proper distance from their mouth, about three or four inches is good. (Note: If you know you are going to have an inexperienced person using a handheld, for a special announcement for example, introduce yourself and show him how you would like him to hold the mic.)

For the pastor with a clip-on mic, known as a wireless lavalier mic, it has to be close enough to the mouth to work effectively. Make sure your pastor clips it high enough on his shirt and that the diaphragm (the receiving part of the mic) is facing up toward his mouth. The mic often gets turned sideways which causes many a sound tech to pull out his hair as he tries to get enough signal.

If your pastor has a head mic, or a Countryman-style wireless mic, placement is key. Have the mic pulled around the ear, even with the mouth, but not so close that it causes a proximity effect (boominess or popping). About one or two inches is a good distance from the mouth. It may help to tape the mic into postion; clear medical tape near the ear helps to keep it at the proper angle. If the mic is too long or short, it's okay to (gently) shape and bend the cabling around the ear.

Be sure that your pastor has enough length of cable at his neck to properly turn his head and keep from disrupting the mic position. Take care of your pastors, make an effort to check in with them, not only to look at the mic but to deepen the relationship, so you can partner together in the gospel.

Chapter Forty-Two

Troubleshooting

It's going to happen to you. You can't escape it. Something isn't going to work right, and you are going to have to fix it. In those moments remember the glorious words of Douglas Adams printed in large friendly letters.

"Don't Panic."

In fact, before you do anything, offer up a quick prayer. I know I've gone rampaging into my system to fix one problem and ended up causing more problems in the process. Just stop for a moment, surrender the situation unto the Lord and pray. Then do your best to think logically. Emotions can go nuts in the heat of the moment. Don't lean on your own understanding, trust in the Lord (Pro. 3:5) and trust in the people God has put around you.

One of my first bosses in sound production, Andy Sykora, had a great phrase concerning troubleshooting that always stuck with me: "Go from the known, to the unknown." Start with whatever piece of gear that you definitely know works and then go backwards from there. Just because you don't hear any sound out of your system, don't assume that your amps are dead.

Start with what you know: is the sound board on? It's quite likely nothing is wrong with the board. Is something muted? Is the master fader down? Is something unplugged? Work your way through each component of your system before you tell the band to abandon ship.

So, be prepared for trouble; it lurks around every corner. One piece of gear can bring down an entire service or event. Knowing the weak links in your system is the key to quick troubleshooting. A messy FOH or stage can be one of those weak links that cause nightmares. (Literally! I've had dreams of death by accidental cable strangulation.)

Keep your cables neat when you set the stage, so that when those troubleshooting moments come, you can easily identify things. Label clearly, keeping in mind that others may need to interpret your system. Make it neat unto the Lord! Even if no one ever sees your organization, do it with excellence. I mean, God loves a neatly rolled over/under XLR cable. (He told me so.)

As prepared as you try to be, you may not be able to swiftly resolve an issue, which honestly, you need to be okay with. You may feel the pressure, but remember that God is sovereign and He knows exactly what's going on. In fact, He's allowed it to happen. How you handle these situations can greatly reflect if your heart is in submission to the will of God.

Do everything you can to resolve issues, work hard to be prepared, and think through every angle; but be ready to move with the Spirit or get out of the way. Remember you're not the one in charge of those 20,000 frequencies anyways. The Spirit will accomplish what is needed, with or without your help.

And always know where your towel is.

How Can I Be Saved?

I have no idea where this book will go and whose hands it might end up in. You may have read this whole book and you're not sure if you are saved. You might have had an idea of what it means to be a Christian, to live a life pleasing to God. And maybe God has brought that to light for you as you've read this book. Or maybe you have never heard the gospel and don't know how to be saved. This is for you.

First we must understand that our sin has separated us from God. God is holy and because of that, God hates sin. God is also just and His justice requires Him to punish sin. The wages of sin is death. (Rom. 6:23) For God to ignore our sin without the required punishment would violate His holiness and justice. So how can we be saved from this punishment and fate, which is ultimately Hell? There has to be a subsitute to stand between the perfect God and imperfect mankind. This subsitute is Jesus Christ, the Son of God.

Jesus takes on the holy wrath of God and clothes us with His righteousness. When God looks at us, he no longer sees our sin, He sees His Son's blood and His righteousness on us. It justifies us with God. This is why Jesus had to die on the cross. We couldn't take on the wrath of God, our due punishment for our sins. Jesus offers us His sacrifice freely and desires all to be saved. So how do we do this?

> If you confess with your mouth that Jesus is Lord and believe in your heart that God raised Him from the dead, you will be saved. For with the heart one believes and is justified, and with the mouth one confesses and is saved... For "everyone who calls on the name of the Lord will be saved." (Rom. 10:9-10,13)

Only if we confess and believe in Jesus Christ do we become saved. And only then does the Holy Spirit come and dwell within us, renewing our mind, soul, and heart which gives us the power to change and to begin to obey and follow God.

If I am completely honest, and because I truly love you and want you to know the joy of being reunited with God and the deep riches of His love and grace, you should know that you can confess with your mouth that Jesus is Lord, but not believe it in your heart (Belief comes from action and belief is a gift from God.) Following Christ might cost everything that you currently hold dear: relationships, material things, your health. When Jesus called His disciples, He asked them to drop everything and just follow, to simply trust Him.

Like the rich young man in Mark 10, there are too many of us who will not follow Christ, because we're holding on to what this world can offer. I beg you to consider what you're forfeiting if you think following Jesus is "a good idea" but don't follow through. Jesus is the only way to salvation. There won't be anything you can do to save yourself, to make yourself right with God. And once you're dead and standing before God, He will either see your sin, or His Son's blood. And if He sees your sin, He will cast you out and into Hell forever. And I love you too much not to tell you this.

> For what does it profit a man if he gains the whole world and loses or forfeits himself? (Luke 9:25)

Glossary

Ballpark – when used in sound, it refers to getting a decent mix together quickly; not spending all day tweaking; no actual sports involved

Band Rider – a list of requirements and requests from a band outlining equipment/technical needs

Bandwidth – the amount of volume or width of a range of frequencies that a speaker is able to output

Cables – those things that actually carry the signal from place to place
    ¼ inch cable – also called a "quarter-inch" cable or "6.3 mm" plug; often used for musical instruments to plug into a direct box; guitarists never seem to have them
    NL4 Cable – or Neutrik/Speakon cables; a cable used to connect speakers, including monitors
    Snake – a collection of four to sixty-four individual long XLR cables combined into one thick cable, used instead of running a billion cables from the sound board to the stage; not actually a part of the reptile family
    XLR – a basic microphone cable named in reference to the wiring: ground (X), left (L), and right (R)

Clipping – when a channel's input level goes beyond it's highest limit and distorts; a red light is involved

Compressor – a device that reduces the dynamic range between the loudest and quietest parts of an audio signal
    Attack – how quickly a compressor activates before reducing a signal after the threshold has been crossed

Compression Rate – refers to the ratio section of a compressor; how much compression is being used

Limiter – when a compressor's ratio is set so high that it barely lets any sound through

Ratio – the knob on a compressor that controls how much a signal is being compressed; for example, a 2:1 ratio is light compression and an 8:1 ratio is heavy compression; known to cause headaches if thought about too much.

Release – how quickly a compressor increases signal once the level has fallen below the threshold

Threshold – the knob on a compressor that controls the level a signal must exceed in order for a compressor to begin to compress

Coverage – refers to the evenness of each level of frequencies throughout the room; basically you want the system to sound the same no matter where you are in the room

Decibels – or dB; a unit used to measure the intensity/volume of sound; used to determine how hard a band rocks

dBA – refers to "A Weight," the volume standard relating to the measurement of sound; there are other weights, but you can ignore them

Direct Box – or DI; converts an instrument cable to an XLR cable; used primarily for acoustic guitars and keyboards

Distortion – when a sound is no longer accurately reproduced due to clipping, the waveform of the signal is not smooth or a sine wave but becomes a square wave; guitars players seem to love it though

Digital Conversion – The process of converting analog audio signals into digital signals

Dynamic Range – the difference in volume in a performance from loud dramatic moments to quiet emotional moments

Effects – devices that alter a sound, such as reverbs or delays

Delay – another magic box that makes a vocal or instrument sound like it's repeating or like a decaying echo

Tap Function – the button that sets the time of delay in milliseconds and allows it to be broken down into a rhythm

Gates – a device that allows only set amounts of signal to be heard below a certain threshold; keeps unwanted ambient sounds out

Range – the knob on a gate that controls the amount of signal released once the gate opens

Reverb – a device within a sound board that makes a vocal or instrument sound like it's in a small room, large hall, or cave

Suck Knob – a mythical knob that causes things to sound better by removing the "suck factor" from the performance

Sustain – the period of time during which a sound remains before it becomes inaudible or silent

Equalization – or EQ; the process of adjusting the frequencies of a particular signal/channel, it changes how something sounds overall

Crossovers – a device within a rack or DSP that controls which frequencies are sent to specific speakers, typically the low frequencies to the subs and the rest to the top boxes

Digital Signal Processor – or DSP; a device contained in a rack that people really, really like to lock up because it has all of the system EQ tuning as well as the routing and output information for all the speakers in the system

EQ Strip – the area on the sound board that controls the EQ for each channel; usually vertical above each channel on an analog board; placement on digital boards vary, but will have physical knobs as well as a digital page component

Parametric EQ – a type of equalizer that changes the frequencies in a broader range (lows, low-mids, high-mids, highs); the primary tool used to EQ; the same as an EQ strip

Graphic EQ – a device that shows the thirty-one bands of frequencies that you can cut or boost to shape the sound, usually used on the main output of a sound board or on monitors

Thumbing – the act of pulling more than one frequency on a Graphic EQ; put your thumb on a frequency and pull the ones immediately next to it; unless you have a tiny thumb…

Q Knob – the part of an equalizer that controls frequency range; a narrow Q grabs only a few frequencies and a wide Q grabs several

High Pass Filter – or HPF; the part of an equalizer that filters out low frequencies while allowing the higher frequencies to pass

Low Pass Filter – or LPF; the part of an equalizer that filters out high frequencies while allowing the lower frequencies to pass; the opposite of HPF

Real Time Analyzing Software – or RTA; software that interfaces with a microphone to measure frequencies and reflections in a room with a sound system

Resonant Frequencies – frequencies that seem to bounce around the room and last for several seconds

Retune/Tune – to set/reset EQ over the sound system

Feedback – when a vocal or instrument mic is so loud that when the signal comes out of the speakers, it goes back into the mic and gets louder, screechier, and more annoying

FOH – or "Front of House;" where the sound board is

Gaff Tape – or gaffer's tape; high quality tape that doesn't leave a residue; used for various reasons in the production world, such as to tape cables down so that people don't trip; the best tape in the world! NOT DUCT TAPE

Gain – usually the first knob on every channel on a sound board; refers to amplifying a signal/channel (see Ch. 8)

    ¾ or -15 Rule – to set your input level around -15 or about ¾ of the way up the meter where zero would be on an analog board; used in setting gain structure

    Solo – a button on a sound board that lets you isolate a channel to listen through headphones; helpful in setting gain structure

Unity – on an analog board: when the fader is at zero on the channel or the input signal has reached zero on it's meter; on amps: when the dial is set to zero or "wide open;" when setting gain structure, the inputs should be averaging zero/unity

Mix – the result of setting the volumes and EQs of various instruments and vocals; most mixes are good, your results may vary

Mics – or microphones

    Condenser Microphone – a fancy, expensive mic that requires 48 volts in order for its diaphragm to function; for example, the SM81 overhead mic or the SM87 vocal mic often used because they sound better than a dynamic mic

    48 Volts – or "phantom power;" a small button typically located at the top of each channel that sends 48 volts down a mic cable to power condenser mics; must be engaged for condenser mics to function; also, it won't kill you if touch the cable while it's active…

    Dynamic Microphones – a basic mic such as the SM57 or SM58

    Talkback Mic – a mic used to talk to the band through the monitors or in the sound system; often used to make fart noises or tell jokes

Monitor – or wedge; a speaker used on stage by performers to hear the performance, or used in the studio to hear what has been recorded

    Avioms – an Ethernet-based monitor system with individual stations for each performer that allows them to choose between a number of channels to create a personal monitor mix; ear buds with a long extension are typically used

    In-Ear Monitor – or IEM; a device used by performers as a personal monitor; consists of a rack-mounted transmitter that receives signal from a monitor send and transmits it to a wireless receiver pack worn on the body, and specific ear buds that connect to the receiver pack; the type of buds used fit inside the ear and block ambient noise allowing the performer to focus on what they need to hear; can also be highly amusing to watch people use for the first time

Moon Gels – little blue pieces of gel that drummers put on their snares and toms (usually on the top) that reduce the resonance; also...they are not candy...don't ask

Outboard Gear – the compressors, graphic EQs, reverbs, and delays controlled through a rack next to the sound board

Patching – the act of plugging a mic cable into a snake or sound board
    1 to 1 – patching in such a way that the channel numbers on the snake do match the corresponding channel numbers on the sound board
    Cross-Patching – patching in such a way that the channel numbers on the snake do not match the corresponding channel numbers on the sound board; usually very confusing and nonsensical

Pre-Fader – a button that allows a signal to be unaffected by the fader position; primarily used for monitor sends

Post-Fader – refers to when the pre-fader button is disengaged; the signal will be affected by the fader position; primarily used for alternate outputs such as a lobby mix

Sibilance – a "hissing" sound on "S's" or high frequencies

Sound Board – or mixing console; that big thing with all lights, knobs, and faders that the church may or may not have spent too much money on
    Analog Board – usually refers to an older sound board that has all the channels and knobs physically laid out
    Digital Board – a newer sound board that has many of the compontents laid out on a screen which are then navigated through digital pages

Aux – a separate submix within a mixing console, often used for monitors

Auxiliary Sends – "aux sends" or just "sends;" usually refers to an output on a sound board that is going to a monitor or another output

Channel – the inputs on a sound board used for instruments, vocals, etc

Faders – those things on the sound board that make the individual vocals and instruments louder; often white or grey, though they can be any color, but if you have a black fader... then it's called a "Darth Fader"

Higher Fader Resolutions – the area ten above and ten below zero on a channel, smaller lines are used; a signal is increased/decreased by only 1 dB

Master Fader – the main output of a sound board which usually controls the left, right, and center outputs; also known as the "Gas!" fader

Main/Left/Right Fader – the main output of a sound board; see also Master Fader

M7cl – a digital sound board made by Yahama

Pre-Amp – located in a sound board; one for every channel to boost the signal

Pre-Fader Listen – or PFL; see Solo

X32 – a digital sound board made by Behringer

Zero – the number zero on each channel or meter; see Unity

Sound Check – the time set aside for the sound engineer to check each channel while the band is on stage

Speaker – a device that converts electrical impulses into sound; that thing that makes all the noise

Amplifier – or amp; what makes a speaker function by "amplifying" a signal

Active Speaker – a speaker containing an amplifier inside that allows it to function

Passive Speaker – a speaker requiring an external amplifier in order to function

Speaker Cone – refers to the the actual speaker component of a speaker or amp box; it's that thing that's shaped like a cone

Subwoofers – or subs; speakers designed to reproduce very low bass frequencies; the big, loud, rumbly speakers that neighbors hate

Top Boxes – speakers that cover the high and mid frequency ranges; the main speakers, excluding the subwoofers

Tweeter – the compontent of a speaker specifically designed to reproduce high frequencies

Sub-Mixers – a small mixer or sound board used to combine several inputs into one or two; for example, a gospel church rolls in with four keyboards and instead of trying to find eight free channels, a sub-mixer will combine those eight down to two to patch into your board

Touch – how hard or dynamically a drummer drums; for instance, excellent jazz drummers are full of it

Vamping/Padding – when a musician plays soft, emotional, ethereal background sounds under the close of a sermon; it's what causes people to respond to an altar call

Notes

Sound in the Gospel

Sound in the Gospel

What People are Saying About
Sound in the Gospel

"Dave is a guy whose skill in his work is exceeded only by his passion for the work. He writes here with conviction and clarity, a modern day "son of Korah" sent by God to the church to help her experience the beauty of God in worship."

J.D. Greear
Pastor of The Summit Church &
62nd President of the Southern Baptist Convention

"It's about time we start talking about this stuff! Dave has dug up some uncomfortable issues and ties in the refreshment of the truth of scripture. This book is a nice tool in navigating the many landscapes of the production world through the lens of the Bible."

Ryan Lampa
FOH for Toby Mac

"*Sound in the Gospel* is a much needed book in today's world of production engineering. The heart is addressed extremely well in this book; a fantastic outline of where we should strive to be spiritually and mentally as engineers. This is extremely close to my heart. Every day is a gift, and Dave has really put the time into properly communicating this with real experiences and loads of applicable scripture."

Tim Spidel
FOH for Plumb & Rush of Fools,
Owner of overFlo Productions

"The Apostle Paul tells us that faith comes by hearing. Sound, then, is an essential part of communication. And when the sound is distorted, so also might the gospel be unclear. The task of the sound engineer, then, is more than twisting knobs and flipping switches. It is deeply rooted in an understanding of the gravity of communicating the truth of God. I'm so thankful for this fine book, which not only provides a very practical primer for the sound engineer, but also brings clarity to exactly what that rarely recognized, but always blamed position is all about. As Dave Wright deftly and theologically points out, the sound engineer's work is an opportunity for the gospel to advance, not only in a congregation or an event, but also within him or herself."

Michael Kelly
Speaker, Author of *Transformational Discipleship*
Director of LifeWay Groups Ministry

"I will say that I believe Dave has brought much needed 'sound doctrine' (pardon the pun) to an area that has been largely ignored. Sound engineers can make or break what happens at weekend services. As a former worship leader, I know very well how important they are to the 'success' of the worship team. Unfortunately they are looked to perform a specific function in a church and little thought is given to them concerning the 'ministry of sound.' For too long we have treated them as a 'production role' as opposed to individuals who are partnered together with other staff/volunteers for the advancement of the gospel. This book is well written and comprehensive in it's content. The scriptural basis (Part 1) is outstanding and challenges individuals who serve in this capacity to see themselves as more than just a 'technical' person but as a participant in the mission of the church."

Pastor David Harrell
New Covenant Church; Greenwood, SC

"Dave has always been one of those unique individuals and friends that always has 100% of his heart and head in the game. This book really shows why those two tools that God gave us must work together to achieve success in and out of the church environment. You can't teach being nice, and without that you will leave a lot of people behind in the ministry."

Andy Sykora
Owner of Custom Audio and Lighting

What People are Saying About Our Ministry

"Dave has immense technical knowledge, a passion for the gospel, and a desire to see media teams trained and discipled in both technical and theological knowledge. The training that he supplies sets a foundation for media teams and why the task of a sound person is so critical, but also immensely challenging. The Sound in the Gospel technical training was designed and applied to the direct needs and desires of our team, and our media technicians. I would not hesitate to recommend Dave with Sound in the Gospel to another church or educational media team."

Robert Smith
Manager of Event Media at The Southern Baptist
Theological Seminary; Louisville, KY

"Dave Wright with Sound in the Gospel helped our church worship services tremendously. Even though he played a background role, the entire church was affected because of his expertise. He was able to take the resources that our church had and steward them for the needs of our ministry. Dave is not just a techie-guru, but he cares about people and the gospel, so that everything he does is 'as unto the Lord.' Dave is a real leader in thinking through the technical aspects of worship with a ministry mindset."

Jared Dragoun
Leader and Pastor at NoHo Church; North Hollywood, CA
(former Worship Pastor at Cornerstone Church; Simi Valley, CA)

"For our sound team and band we were at a plateau and stagnate situation. It seemed the life, excitement, and joy had been expelled. At the right time, I came across Sound in the Gospel and it was exactly what we needed and desired. We needed to hear the gospel as it applied to our sound team to confront our sin, how to exalt Jesus Christ (as a sound tech), and then how to replicate and disciple. There was so much wrapped up in that seminar that has changed us. Then we were encouraged through the thorough resetting of our sound system and the personal sound training on the basics which we were lacking. We are very grateful and thankful for this ministry. We no longer turn knobs blindly."

Ben Roberts
Friendship Baptist Church; Statesboro, GA

"We brought in Dave with Sound in the Gospel to be our FOH for our student weekend at church with leaders such as Matt Papa and Leeland. Not only did he run well for them, he also taught us in the process. Immediately following the conference, Dave held a workshop for our audio guys. What a blessing it is to have someone teach your team of audio techs from a Biblical world view and explain their job in light of the gospel. He hits the heart of the matter before training in the practical. Needless to say, I would highly recommned bringing Sound in the Gospel into your church, you will not regret it!"

Josh Sanders
Worship Pastor at Tri-Cities Baptist Church; Gray, TN

About the Author

"Magic Dave" Wright has been working in sound production for over fourteen years. He began his journey studying under sound guru Paul Rice and has had the privilege of working with many talented sound engineers and musicians.

When he's not working his mojo on sound systems, he spends his time battling Sectoids on X-Com and flying RC airplaines. He loves playing piano and guitar as well as doodling with sharpies. He also loves playing board games with his wife, Bea, and making his cats and dog crazy.

Dave does all Sound in the Gospel seminars and training personally, although occasionally his wife accompanies him as Patch Monkey and moral support. If you ask him any question, the answer will always be, "42."

Dave and Bea also run an artist community project called NEBTHOS that strives to inspire the artists in the church through creative events and publishing books.

Find out more at www.NEBTHOS.com

And Another Thing...

If this book has helped you in any way (Praise God!),
please share it with someone. Stick it under your
sound board so that it will always be nearby
to remind you to share what you've learned.

And hey, this book was self-published! YAY!
And right now the marketing plan is—YOU.
Yup, you.
And we believe in you!

So here's all the social media nonsense.

www.soundinthegospel.com

www.facebook.com/soundinthegospel

www.twitter.com/itsallaboutgain

Be on the lookout for more content and resources
from Sound in the Gospel!

And if we can be of assistance to your ministry through
system restoration, consulting, training, or seminars,
please email us at:

info@soundinthegospel.com

Coming soon from Magic Dave

"Gaming in the Gospel: when just one more turn isn't enough"

www.gaminginthegospel.com

Coming in 2019!

More Books Published by

www.nebthos.com

Fire Within

Fire Within: 31 life lessons on evangelism, discipleship and the gospel

Fire Within is a devotional/collection of stories based on author Jesse Eisenhour's experience as a street evangelist with Time to Revive. He has been sharing the gospel in cities across the country by simply asking people, "How can I pray for you?" And now Jesse Eisenhour wants you to find the fire within yourself to reach out to your neighborhood, coworkers, or strangers and start sharing the gospel.

If you've ever struggled with how to make evangelism a part of your daily life, *Fire Within* will help give you a clear picture of what a lifestyle of evangelism could look like. But beware! Reading this book might change your life FOREVER!

Available at
amazon.com

Printed in the USA
CPSIA information can be obtained
at www.ICGtesting.com
LVHW010335130824
788107LV00003B/211